Walk in the Light Series

The Law and Grace

Examining the Relevance and Application of the Torah to All Believers

Todd D. Bennett

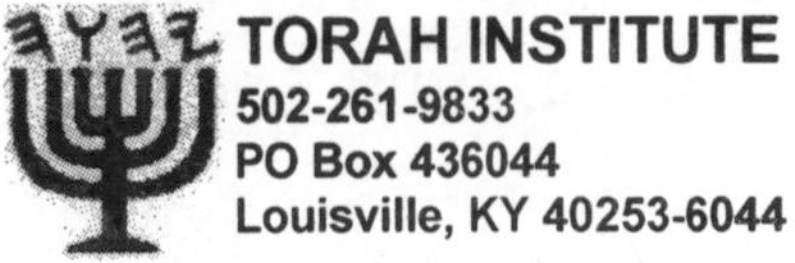

Shema Yisrael Publications

The Law and Grace
Examining the Relevance and Application of the Torah to All Believers

First printing 2006, Second Printing 2009

For information write: Shema Yisrael Publications, 123 Court Street, Herkimer, New York 13350.

ISBN: 0-9768659-3-9
Library of Congress Number: 2006909649

Printed in the United States of America.

Please visit our website for other titles:

www.shemayisrael.net

For information regarding publicity for author interviews call (866) 866-2211

The Law and Grace

Examining the Relevance and Application of the Torah to All Believers

"For while the Torah was given through Mosheh,
grace and truth came through Yahushua the Messiah"

John (Yahanan) 1:17

Table of Contents

Acknowledgements
Introduction i
Chapter 1 In the Beginning 1
Chapter 2 The Law 8
Chapter 3 The Pharisees and the Law 20
Chapter 4 Messiah and the Torah 26
Chapter 5 Messiah and the Pharisees 32
Chapter 6 Messiah Teaches Torah 46
Chapter 7 The Disciples and the Torah 55
Chapter 8 Shaul and the Torah 63
Chapter 9 The Teachings of Shaul 69
Chapter 10 The Jerusalem Council 75
Chapter 11 The Torah and the Covenants 99
Chapter 12 Grace 119
Chapter 13 Blessings and Curses 128
Chapter 14 Christianity and the Torah 142
Chapter 15 Lawlessness 155
Chapter 16 The Walk of Faith 165
Chapter 17 In The End 172
Endnotes 178
Appendix A - Tanak Hebrew Names
Appendix B - The Walk in the Light Series Overview
Appendix C - The Shema
Appendix D - The Shema Yisrael Foundation

Acknowledgments

I must first and foremost acknowledge my Creator, Redeemer and Savior who opened my eyes and showed me the Light. He never gave up on me even when, at times, it seemed that I gave up on Him. He is ever patient and truly awesome. His blessings, mercies and love endure forever and my gratitude and thanksgiving cannot be fully expressed in words.

Were it not for the patience, prayers, love and support of my beautiful wife Janet, and my extraordinary children Morgan and Shemuel, I would never have been able to accomplish this work. They gave me the freedom to pursue the vision and dreams that my Heavenly Father placed within me and for that I am so very grateful. I love them all more than they will ever know.

Loving thanks to my father for his helpful comments and editing. He tirelessly watched and held things together at my office while I was away traveling, researching, speaking and writing.

Introduction

"[20] Everyone who does evil hates the light, and will not come into the light for fear that his deeds will be exposed. [21] But whoever lives by the truth comes into the light, so that it may be seen plainly that what he has done has been done through God."

John 3:20-21 NIV

This book entitled "The Law and Grace" is part of a larger body of educational work called the "Walk in the Light" series. As such it is built upon a number of other topics and ideally the reader would have read about Paganism in Christianity as well as the need for restoration. Due to the importance of the subject of this text, and each volume in the series, I have attempted to present them in such a fashion that they can stand alone. In order to do this I have used extensive annotations and I would encourage the reader to review the endnotes in order to better understand the present subject and fill in some gaps which may appear in the text.

This book, and the entire series, were written as a result of my search for the truth. Having grown up in a major protestant Christian denomination since I was a small child, I had been steeped in doctrine which often

times seemed to contradict the very words contained within the Scriptures. I always considered myself to be a Christian, although I never took the time to research the origins of Christianity or to understand exactly what the term Christian really meant. I simply grew up believing that Christianity was right and every other religion was wrong or in some way deficient.

Yet, my beliefs were founded on more than simply blind faith. I had experienced a "living God," my life had been transformed by a loving Redeemer and I had been filled with a powerful Spirit. I knew that I was on the right track, but again, I continually felt something was lacking. I was certain that there was something more to this religion called Christianity; not in terms of a different God, but in terms of what composed this belief system to which I subscribed, and this label which I wore like a badge.

Throughout my Christian walk I experienced many highs and some lows, but along the way I never felt like I fully understood what my faith was all about. Sure, I knew that "Jesus died on the cross for my sins" and that I needed to believe in my heart and confess with my mouth in order to "be saved." I "asked Jesus into my heart" when I was a child and sincerely believed in what I had done, but something always felt like it was missing. As I grew older, I found myself progressing through different denominations, each time learning and growing, always adding some pieces to the puzzle, but never seeing the entire picture.

College ministry brought me into contact with the baptism of the Holy Spirit and more charismatic assemblies yet, while these people seemed to practice a more complete

faith than those in my previous denominations, many of my original questions remained unanswered and even more questions arose. It seemed that at each new step in my faith I added a new adjective to the already ambiguous label "Christian." I went from being a mere Christian to a Full Gospel, New Testament, Charismatic, Spirit Filled, Born Again Christian; although I could never get away from the lingering uneasiness that something was still missing.

For instance, when I read Matthew 7:21-23 I always felt uncomfortable. In that Scripture, the Messiah says: "*Not everyone who says to Me, Lord, Lord, will enter the kingdom of heaven, but he who does the will of My Father Who is in heaven. Many will say to Me on that day, Lord, Lord, have we not prophesied in Your name and driven out demons in Your name and done many mighty works in Your name? And then I will say to them openly (publicly), I never knew you; depart from Me, you who act wickedly [disregarding My commands].*" The Amplified Bible.

This passage of Scripture always bothered me because it sounded an awful lot like the modern day Christian Church, in particular, the charismatic churches which I had been attending where the gifts of the Spirit were operating. According to the Scripture passage it was not the people who ***believed*** in the spiritual manifestations that were being rejected, it was those who were ***actually doing*** them. I would think that this would give every Christian pause for concern.

First of all "in that day" there are ***many*** people who will be calling the Messiah "Lord." They will also be performing incredible spiritual feats in His Name. Ultimately though, the Messiah will openly and publicly

tell them to depart from Him. He will tell them that He never knew them and specifically He defines them by their actions, which is the reason for their rejection; they acted wickedly or lawlessly. In short, they disobeyed His commandments. Also, it seems very possible that while they thought they were doing these things in His Name, they were not, because they may have never known His Name. In essence, they did not know Him and He did not know them.

I think that many Christians are haunted by this Scripture because they do not understand who it applies to or what it means. If they were truly honest they must admit that there is no other group on the face of the planet that it can refer to except for the "Christian Church."

Ultimately, my search for answers brought me right back to the starting point of my faith. I was left with the question: "What is the origin and substance of this religion called Christianity?" I was forced to examine the very foundations of my faith and many of the beliefs to which I subscribed and to test them against the truth of the Scriptures.

What I found out was nothing short of earth shattering. I experienced a personal parapettio, which is the moment in Greek tragedies where the hero realizes that everything he knew was wrong. I discovered that many of the foundations of my faith were not rocks of truth, but rather the sands of lies, deception, corruption and paganism. I saw the Scripture passage in the prophesy of Jeremiah (Yirmeyahu) come true right before my eyes. In many translations, this passage reads: "*O LORD, my strength and my fortress, My refuge in the day of affliction, The Gentiles shall come to You from the ends of the earth and*

say, "Surely our fathers have inherited lies, worthlessness and unprofitable things. Will a man make gods for himself, which are not gods?" Jeremiah (Yirmeyahu) 16:19-20 NKJV

I discovered that I had inherited lies and false doctrines from the fathers of my faith. I discovered that the faith which I had been steeped in had made gods which were not gods, and I saw very clearly how many could say "Lord, Lord" and not really know the Messiah or do the will of the Father, because they had actually rejected His commandments. I discovered that many of these lies were not just minor discrepancies but critical errors which could possibly have the effect of keeping me out of the New Jerusalem if I continued to practice them. (Revelation 21:27; 22:15).

While part of the problem stemmed from false doctrines which have crept into the Christian religion, it also had to do with anti-Semitism imbedded throughout the centuries which intentionally stripped the Christian religion of anything perceived as "Jewish." I even discovered translation errors in the very Scriptures that I was basing may beliefs upon. A good example is the next verse from the Prophet Jeremiah (Yirmeyahu) where most translations read: *"Therefore behold, I will this once cause them to know, I will cause them to know My hand and My might; and they shall know that My Name is the LORD."* Jeremiah (Yirmeyahu) 16:21 NKJV.

Could our Heavenly Father really be telling us that His Name is "the LORD"? This is a title, not a name and by the way, won't many people be crying out "Lord, Lord" and be told that He never knew them? It is obvious that you should know someone's name in order to have a relationship with them. How could you possibly say

that you know someone if you do not even know their name. So then we must ask: "What is the Name of our Heavenly Father?" The answer to this seeming mystery lies just beneath the surface of the translated text. In fact, if most people took the time to read the translators notes in the front of their Bible they would easily discover the problem.

You see the Name of our Creator is found in the Scriptures almost 7,000 times, although long ago a false doctrine was perpetrated regarding speaking the Name. It was determined that the Name either could not, or should not, be pronounced, and therefore it was replaced. Thus, over the centuries the Name of the Creator which was given to us so that we could know Him and be, not only His children, but also His friends, (Isaiah 41:8, James 2:23, John 15:15) was suppressed and altered. You will now find people using descriptions, titles and variations to replace the Name such as: God, Lord, Adonai, Jehovah and Ha Shem ("The Name") in place of the actual Name which was declared in Scriptures. What a tragedy and what a mistake!

One of the Ten Commandments, also known as the Ten Words, specifically instructs us not to take the Name of the Creator "in vain" and "*He will not hold him guiltless who takes His name in vain.*" (Exodus 20:7). Most Christians have been taught that this simply warns of using the Name lightly or in the context of swearing or in some other disrespectful manner. This certainly is one aspect of the commandment, but if we look further into the Hebrew word for vain - שוא (pronounced shaw) we find that it has a deeper meaning in the sense of "desolating, uselessness, emptiness, nothingness or naught."

Therefore, we have been warned not only to avoid using the Name lightly or disrespectfully, but also not to bring it to naught, which is exactly what has been done over the centuries. The Name of our Creator which we have the privilege of calling on and praising has been suppressed to the point where most Believers do not even know the Name, let alone use it.

This sounds like a conspiracy of cosmic proportions and it is. Anyone who believes in the Scriptures must understand that there is a battle between good and evil. There is a Prince of Darkness, Satan, who understands very well the battle which has been raging since the creation of time. He will do anything to distract or destroy those searching for the truth, and he is very good at what he does. He is the Master of Deception and the Father of Lies, and he does not want the truth to be revealed. His goal is to steal, kill and destroy. (John 10:10). The enemy has operated both openly and behind the scenes over the centuries to infect, deceive, distract and destroy Believers with false doctrines. He truly is a wolf in sheep's clothing, and his desire is to rob the Believer of blessings and life.

As you read this book I hope that you will see how he has worked his deception regarding the subjects of the Law and Grace. We are given wonderful promises in the Scriptures concerning blessings for those who obey the commandments. Sadly, many Believers have been robbed of those blessings due to false doctrines which teach them to <u>not</u> keep the commandments, thus turning them into lawless individuals. Their belief is not followed by righteous works thereby making their faith empty and, to some extent, powerless.

My hope is that every reader has an eye opening experience and is forever changed. I sincerely believe that the truths which are contained in this book and the entire "Walk in the Light" series are essential to avoid the great deception which is being perpetrated upon those who profess to believe in, and follow the Holy One of Yisra'el.

This book, and the entire series, is intended for anyone who is searching for the truth. Depending upon your particular religion, customs and traditions, you may find some of the information to be contrary to the doctrines and teachings which you have read or heard throughout your life. Please realize however, that none of the information is meant to criticize anyone or any faith, but merely to reveal truth.

The information contained in this book should stir up some things or else there would be no reason to have written it in the first place. The ultimate question is whether the contents align with the Scriptures and the will of the Creator. My goal is to strip away the layers of tradition which many of us have inherited and get to the core of the faith which is described in the Scriptures commonly called "The Bible."

This book should challenge your thinking and your beliefs and hopefully aid you on your search for truth. My prayer for you is that of the Apostle Paul, properly known as Shaul, in his letter to the Ephesian assembly that: "[17]. . . *the Father of esteem, would give you a spirit of wisdom and revelation in the knowledge of Him,* [18] *the eyes of your understanding being enlightened so that you know what is the expectation of His calling, and what are the riches of the esteem of His inheritance in the set-apart ones,*[19] *and what is the*

exceeding greatness of His power toward us who are believing, according to the working of His mighty strength." Ephesians 1:17-19 The Scriptures.

I

In the Beginning

Few matters evoke a more passionate response than when a Christian is confronted with the notion that they must obey the Law. In fact, anyone familiar with Christianity would likely find the title of this book to be an oxymoron since "the Law" and "grace" are often treated as two diametrically opposed concepts.

As we shall discover, the title is actually a misnomer because neither of the words "Law" or "grace" accurately reflect the true Scriptural concepts which they portend to represent. Notwithstanding, many have been taught, and sincerely believe, that "the Law" has been replaced, or rather, superseded by grace. The essence of this book is to demonstrate the fallacy of that notion and its subsequent devastating impact upon Christian doctrine.

Christians look to Jesus Christ as the "founder" of their religion, although few understand that His correct Hebrew Name is Yahushua.[1] They believe that He is the promised Messiah[2] and therefore look to His life and teachings to guide them in their spiritual journey. Many who endeavor down that path of faith begin with the Good News according to John, commonly called the

Gospel of John. After all, every American sports fan is familiar with John 3:16: "*For God so loved the world that He gave His only begotten Son, that whoever believes in Him should not perish but have everlasting life.*"

Having gleaned that extraordinary truth from the writings of John, better known as Yahanan[3] in Hebrew, it only makes sense to look further into the text for additional instruction. In fact, it helps to start at the very beginning. It is no coincidence that this manuscript starts out with the very same words as the Book of Genesis, also known as Beresheet[4] which means "*In the beginning.*" We are told that this One called Yahushua was the Word and the Light.

The purpose of the writer was intentional because without an understanding of what happened "in the beginning" there is no way to appreciate the work of Yahushua. That is why we must first go back to the beginning to fully understand the dynamics involved in the great controversy concerning "the Law" and grace because it is essential to the ministry and purpose of the Messiah.

After the creation account we are told that the Creator of the Universe, known as YHWH Elohim,[5] gave the man, Adam, a specific purpose. He was placed in the Garden of Eden "*to tend and keep it.*" Beresheet 2:15 NKJV. The Hebrew word for "tend" is abad (עבד) and the Hebrew word for "keep" is shamar (שמר). Both of these words are verbs and they involve action. These concepts are very important as we shall see throughout our discussion and another way of describing Adam's mission is "*to work and to watch*" or "*to do and to guard.*"

After we are told what Adam was <u>to do</u> in the Garden

we are then told of one specific commandment which he was given. The Scriptures record: "[16] *And YHWH Elohim commanded the man, saying, 'Of every tree of the garden you may freely eat;* [17] *but of the tree of the knowledge of good and evil you shall not eat, for in the day that you eat of it you shall surely die.'*" Beresheet 2:16-17. Now this was by no means the only command given to mankind, but it happened to be the first one that was transgressed – that is why we are provided the specific details of this particular command. Adam was surely given instructions concerning his duties and what was expected of him as he and his Creator walked and fellowshipped together in the Garden.[6]

It is essential to recognize that mankind was given commandments from the beginning - they were not new at Mount Sinai. Many people believe that it was not until Moses (Mosheh)[7] went up and received the Ten Commandments that the commandments of YHWH were actually revealed to mankind. This is not true and as we examine the Scriptures it is plain to see that from Adam through Mosheh there was always a righteous line that knew and followed the commandments of YHWH. What was new at Sinai was the fact that those commandments were codified and incorporated into the Covenant made with Yisrael.[8]

As a result of this misplaced thinking people often view Mosheh and Yahushua in opposition to one another in the same way that they pit "the Law" against grace. This results primarily from a failure to understand what is commonly referred to as "the Law." Another reason is because of faulty translations of the Scriptures which

support bad doctrines. This promotes erroneous teachings which, in turn, lead to flawed beliefs.

An example of a poor translation can be seen in the very text that we previously mentioned – Yahanan. In a popular English translation of the Scriptures we are told the following:

> "[1] *In the beginning was the Word, and the Word was with God, and the Word was God.* [2] *He was in the beginning with God.* [3] *All things were made through Him, and without Him nothing was made that was made.* [4] *In Him was life, and the life was the light of men.* [5] *And the light shines in the darkness, and the darkness did not comprehend it.* [6] *There was a man sent from God, whose name was John.* [7] *This man came for a witness, to bear witness of the Light, that all through Him might believe.* [8] *He was not that Light, but was sent to bear witness of that Light.* [9] *That was the true Light which gives light to every man coming into the world.* [10] *He was in the world, and the world was made through Him, and the world did not know Him.* [11] *He came to His own, and His own did not receive Him.* [12] *But as many as received Him, to them He gave the right to become children of God, to those who believe in His name:* [13] *who were born, not of blood, nor of the will of the flesh, nor of the will of man, but of God.* [14] *And the Word became flesh and dwelt among us, and we beheld His glory, the glory as of the only begotten of the Father, full of grace and truth.*[15] *John bore witness of Him and cried out, saying, 'This was*

He of whom I said, He who comes after me is preferred before me, for He was before me.' [16] *And of His fullness we have all received, and grace for grace.* [17] *For the law was given through Moses, but grace and truth came through Jesus Christ." Yahanan 1:1-17 NKJV.*

The above passage of Scripture is often used to support the belief that grace replaced "the Law." This is despite the fact that the text takes us right back *to the beginning*. For some reason many Christians believe that something was drastically changed when *the Word became flesh*. Part of the problem rests in the translation of this passage – in particular the word "but" which is found in verse 17 in both the King James Version and the New King James Version.

In English grammar the word "but" is a conjunction which facilitates the transition between independent clauses by conveying a sense that the meaning of the second clause is going to be different from the sense expressed in the first clause. Therefore, most people who read the verse get the distinct impression that Yahanan is telling us that grace is different than "the Law" which leads to the mistaken belief that grace has surpassed or replaced "the Law."

The trouble with this understanding is that the word "but" is not found in the Greek manuscripts used to translate the text into English. The word has been inserted into the English translations by translators who apparently *thought* that they were clarifying the intent of the author. Through their mistranslation they have seemingly placed "the Law" in direct opposition and conflict with grace.

Other modern translations simply insert a

semicolon instead of the "but" which is more accurate although still vague. A precise rendering of this verse reads as follows:

> *"For while the Torah was given through Mosheh, grace and truth came through Yahushua the Messiah."*

The first thing that will stand out to most readers is the name change of Moses (Mosheh) and Jesus (Yahushua). The subject of Names is so broad and important that it cannot be dealt with in this discussion and is handled separately in the Walk in the Light series book entitled "Names."

The next difference which should stand out is the use of the word Torah in place of the word "law." Much of this book will focus on the meaning and significance of the Torah. The Torah, which is often translated as "the Law" in most English translations of the Bible, is more accurately described as "the instructions of Elohim" and is also referred to as "*truth*" in the Scriptures. (Psalms 119:151).

With this information it should be obvious that the Torah, <u>*which is truth*</u>, is not and cannot be opposed to grace. Rather while the truth (Torah) was given through Mosheh, grace **and** truth (Torah) came through Yahushua who is the Word and the Light ***from the beginning.***

As will be demonstrated throughout this book translators have, at times, changed certain texts of Scripture to fit their own theological paradigm rather than modifying their preconceived theology to conform to the true meaning contained within the manuscripts.[9] I have observed that there is a profound misunderstanding of

the Torah within the Christian religion which has led to erroneous doctrines and confusing interpretations as men strive to fit a square peg into a round hole. Without a proper understanding of the Torah you will never understand the "Old Testament," let alone the teachings of the Messiah or other writings in the "New Testament" - better known as the Messianic Scriptures.[10]

2

The Law

Before proceeding any further, it is important to elaborate on the error of translating the Hebrew word "Torah" into the English language as "Law." The word "Law" is commonly used in Christendom without much understanding of what is actually meant by the term. When we hear the word "Law" it typically stirs emotions and thoughts of police, judges, fines, punishment and even prison. This undeniable reality often tainted my perception of the Torah as I studied Christian doctrine and sadly this is not the only instance where translators have greatly influenced how we read, understand and interpret the Scriptures.

The use of the word "Law" rather than the word Torah is yet another example of the distortion of a fundamental concept in the Scriptures which has resulted from inaccurate translations. In a very general sense, the word Torah is used to refer to the first five books of the Scriptures which some call the Pentateuch. While some refer to the entire "Old Testament" as the Torah, the "Old Testament" is more properly known as the Tanak[11] which includes the Torah, the Prophets (Nebi'im) and the writings (Kethubim).

The word Torah (תורה) in Hebrew means *utterance, teaching, instruction or revelation from Elohim.* It comes from horah (הורה) which means ***to direct, to teach*** and derives from the stem yara (ירה) which means to **shoot** or **throw.** Therefore there are two aspects to the word Torah: 1) aiming or pointing in the right direction, and 2) movement in that direction. This gives a much different sense than the word "Law."

When showing the spelling of certain Hebrew words thus far I have used modern Hebrew characters although it is important to point out that the modern Hebrew language consists of a character set which is vastly different from the original language. The current Hebrew language uses characters which were developed around the 6th century BCE and adopted during the Babylonian exile.

The language which was originally spoken and written by Hebrews is now referred to as Ancient Hebrew or Paleo-Hebrew. Although it went through a number of changes over the centuries we are able to discern the original symbols and unlike modern Hebrew, these early Semitic languages used pictographs which actually resemble their meanings.

In modern Hebrew the word Torah is spelled תורה and in Ancient Hebrew it would look something like this: 𐤕𐤅𐤓𐤄. When these pictographs were joined together they became words with meanings that derived from the individual symbols. I find it particularly interesting in my research and studies to look at the original symbols of a word to derive its meaning.

The word Torah is a combination of four symbols:

† - a cross which means "to seal or covenant."

Y - a nail or peg which means "to add or secure."

𐤓 - a head which means "a person, the head or the highest."

𐤄 - a person with hands raised which means "to reveal or behold or what comes from."

Combining the meanings of these symbols gives us a profound definition of the word "Torah" as "what comes from the man nailed to the cross" or "behold the man who secures the covenant."

"Because the Hebrew word for sin - cha-ta (חטא) means to miss the target – the word Torah becomes vital if we don't want to miss the purpose and fulfillment of our life. These concepts of teaching and helping to fulfill the purpose of your life is found in Proverbs 1:8 where Scripture tells us not to forsake the Torah (teaching, direction) of your mother. [Elohim] with the heart of a loving mother, wants us to know how to hit the target, how to be complete in life. The Torah points out the real goals of life. The Torah shows us how to hit the mark and this agrees with the word picture for Torah, that shows us where the Torah comes from."[12]

It is quite evident that the word "Law" is an inadequate and incorrect translation of the word Torah. According to my understanding of the etymology of the word Torah it is more accurately defined as:

> *"the instructions of Elohim for mankind given in the garden and passed on through generations until it was codified by Mosheh and fullfilled through the life, death, resurrection and reign of*

the Messiah."

The Torah contains <u>instructions</u>, <u>guidance</u> and <u>direction</u> for those who desire to live righteous, set apart lives in accordance with the will of Elohim. While these instructions were written on scrolls by Mosheh they ultimately are written by the Almighty on the hearts of Believers.

The word "instruction" clearly has a much different connotation than the word "Law." Parents instruct their children and guide their paths to keep them safe so that they can grow up healthy and blessed. While they clearly have rules for their household - those rules are administered in love. Governments and man-made institutions create laws which must be obeyed under threat of punishment. Those who disobey the laws of man are subject to consequences such as fines, imprisonment and even death. Some societies are humane and fair in their implementation of their laws while others are cruel and despotic. Therefore, the experience that a person has had with man-made laws, along with the sense of justice that they perceive from those laws, will likely be carried over to their view of "the Law" in the Scriptures.

It is the use of the vague word "Law" instead of the specific word "Torah" which creates the problem alluded to at the beginning of this chapter. When people read about the "Law of God" they immediately attribute certain perceptions and emotions to the concept based upon their experiences with the "law of man."

This is particularly distressing since the word Torah is rendered in both the Septuagint (LXII), which is the Greek translation of the Hebrew Tanak, and the Greek manuscripts of the Messianic Scriptures using

the word nomos (νομοσ). The word nomos (νομοσ) specifically refers to the Torah and maintains the same sense of "instruction" but when it is translated as "law" in English it loses that meaning. Thus we see that both the Hebrew and Greek words which refer to the "instructions of the Almighty" have been consistently and erroneously translated as "Law" in the English translations of the Bible.

Torah (תורה) is a unique word which has a much more specific connotation, although it too is subject to multiple meanings. As previously mentioned, the Torah is often considered to be the first five books contained within the Hebrew and Christian Scriptures. They were written by Mosheh and collectively they are often referred to as "The Torah." Traditionally these texts are contained in a single scroll known as a "Torah Scroll." The names of the five different "books," or rather seferim, are transliterated from their proper Hebrew names as follows: Beresheet (Genesis), Shemot (Exodus), Vayiqra (Leviticus), Bemidbar (Numbers) and Devarim (Deuteronomy).

Traditionally it is held that there are 613 commandments, also known as mitzvot (מצוות), which are found within the Torah. The Sages teach that there are 248 positive commandments which they say equals the number of important organs in the body. There are 365 negative commandments which they say equals the number of sinews in the body. The total number of commandments (613) equals the total number of sinews and organs which make up a man. This symbolizes the

fact that man was created to obey Elohim and perform His will.

Some go further and divide the commandments into three different categories: 1) moral, 2) ceremonial, and 3) civil. I think it is a serious mistake to attempt to number or categorize the instructions because there is no provision in the Scriptures for such an act and doing so allows men to minimize and disregard various commands based upon their categorization.

Regardless of these different classes or the actual number of commandments, it is clear that not all of the commandments apply to all people. For those desirous of learning and obeying the commandments they must determine which commandments actually apply to them before they can know which ones they must obey. For instance, there are specific instructions which apply to Cohens, Levites, men, women, husbands, fathers, wives, mothers, children and neighbors. The Torah provides instructions to all people so that they may know how to live righteously before their Creator depending upon their particular position in life.

This has always been the case and the Torah was not created exclusively for the Yisraelites at Mt. Sinai. The Torah existed from the very beginning when Adam enjoyed intimate fellowship with his Creator in the garden called Eden.

After Adam was expelled from the garden he still knew what was considered to be righteous conduct and he passed that knowledge to his children. Abel made offerings which were pleasing to the Almighty while Cain did not. The

earth was later judged because mankind was not living according to the instructions of the Almighty. Noah and his family were saved because he was a righteous man who obeyed his Creator. The son of Noah, Shem, carried on the righteous line and some believe that he taught Avraham (Abraham) the Torah.

The Scriptures clearly record that Avraham obeyed the Torah. In Beresheet 26:4-5 we read when Elohim appeared to Isaac and said: "[4] *in your seed all the nations of the earth shall be blessed;* [5] *because Avraham obeyed My voice and kept My charge, My commandments, My statutes, and My Torah.*" Notice that the Torah is treated separately and distinctly from things such as charge – mishmeret (משמרת), commandments – mitzvot (מצוות) and statutes – chuqote (חקות). Avraham kept (shamar) not only the Torah, but also the charge, the commandments and the statutes and ordinances of Elohim. He surely taught the Torah to his children who knew the Ways of their father's Elohim. The righteous ones in the Tanak all obeyed the Torah which was eventually codified by Mosheh when Yisrael became a nation which was about to receive the promises of Avraham when they entered into covenant with Elohim.

Many Christians make the critical mistake of thinking that the Yisraelites were saved by their obedience to the Torah which is completely false. They are further taught that the Messiah freed us from the curse of the Torah and now people are saved by grace. This paradigm has absolutely no basis in fact. The Torah never saved anybody. In fact, the only transgression which a sacrifice would cover according to the Torah was for unintentional sin. There was no provision for intentional sin other

than being "cut off" from the Assembly, qahal (קהל) in Hebrew, which most assuredly meant death. (Bemidbar 15:22-31).

The Torah was specifically for those who believed - whether they were native born Yisraelites or foreigners who wanted to join the community of Yisrael. "*You shall have one Torah for him who sins unintentionally, for him who is native-born among the children of Yisrael and for the stranger who dwells among them.*" Bemidbar 15:29. It is much more than a written list of do's and don'ts - it is the instruction given by the Almighty to a people who desire to walk with Him, live with Him and serve Him in His Kingdom. It goes beyond our four dimensional physical universe that we observe in our daily lives, it is spiritual - yet visible through those who allow the instructions to penetrate their lives and permeate into their very being.[13]

As we already learned the Psalms, more accurately know as Tehillim in Hebrew, define the Torah as truth. "*Your righteousness is an everlasting righteousness, and Your Torah is truth.*" Tehillim 119:142. As a Christian I never looked at the Torah as truth. I grew up believing that the Law was for the "Jews"[14] while Christians had been delivered from the bondage that resulted from being "under the Law." I was taught that the Law was too difficult for any man to obey, except for Jesus, Who lived a perfect life so that He could then do away with the Law and free all mankind by ushering in a new dispensation of grace.[15] This was a paradigm which I inherited and I was provided certain Scripture passages which appeared, at first glance, to support that understanding.

The only problem with this belief is that it is actually not supported by the Scriptures. No doubt,

you can find some select passages, most likely from the writings of Paul (Shaul),[16] to sustain this position but as we shall see later in this book, those Scriptures are usually misunderstood or mistranslated to fit within the preconceived theology that "Jesus replaced the Law with grace."[17]

The notion that the Torah is too difficult or impossible to keep implicitly infers that the Elohim of the "Old Testament"[18] or rather the Tanak, was sadistic enough to compel Yisrael to obey something which they were unable to obey.[19] This is not the nature of my Elohim nor is it the nature of the Elohim of the Scriptures named YHWH.[20] (From this point onward I will use YHWH when referring to the Name of Elohim commonly spelled יהוה in modern Hebrew).

The Torah was never considered to be a burden by the Yisraelites; rather it was thought to be a special gift, a treasure, to a people who were chosen to live set apart lives. (Tehellim 119:162). Yisrael was supposed to be a nation of priests (Shemot 19:6) and the Torah provided them with the instructions necessary to live righteous lives as we read in Sefer Devarim: "*Then it will be righteousness for us, if we are careful to observe all these commandments before YHWH our Elohim, as He has commanded us.*" Devarim 6:25.

The notion that the instructions of YHWH were somehow burdensome or oppressive flies in the face of history and the express teachings in the Scriptures. To begin, the Torah was given to Yisrael <u>after</u> they were freed from slavery. The instructions were given to free people who were delivered from opression. These instructions were not meant to place Yisrael back into bondage. Both the deliverance and the instructions were free gifts given

by a loving Husband to His Bride – Yisrael.

Further, Yisrael was never forced to obey the Torah - they willingly agreed to obey the Torah after they had been delivered from slavery. If they had agreed while they were still slaves, it may have been viewed as if they did so under duress. Instead, YHWH waited until they were free to offer them His Torah. "[7] *So Mosheh came and called for the elders of the people, and laid before them all these words which YHWH commanded him.* [8] *Then all the people answered together and said, '**All that YHWH has spoken we will do.**'"* Shemot 19:7-8. This was the same as when a bride says "I do."

YHWH specifically instructs His people: "[20] *When your son asks you in time to come, saying, 'What is the meaning of the testimonies, the statutes, and the judgments which YHWH our Elohim has commanded you?'* [21] *then you shall say to your son: 'We were slaves of Pharaoh in Egypt, and YHWH brought us out of Egypt with a mighty hand;* [22] *and YHWH showed signs and wonders before our eyes, great and severe, against Egypt, Pharaoh, and all his household.* [23] *Then He brought us out from there, that He might bring us in, to give us the land of which He swore to our fathers.* [24] ***And YHWH commanded us to observe all these statutes, to fear YHWH our Elohim, for our good always, that He might preserve us alive, as** it is this day.'"* Devarim 6:20-24.

A fundamental commandment concerning the Torah is that: "*You shall not add to the word which I command you, nor take from it, that you may keep the commandments of YHWH your Elohim which I command you.*" Devarim 4:2. Again in Devarim 12:32 we read: "*Whatever I command you, be careful to observe it; you shall not add to it nor take away from it.*" The word translated as keep and observe is the same

word in Hebrew - shamar (שמר) and it means: "*to guard, to protect, to hedge about.*" It is the same commandment given to Adam and we cannot guard and obey the Torah if we add to it or take away from it.

This was at the crux of the disobedience in the garden. Adam was commanded "not to eat" but when confronted by the serpent, the woman added to the Torah by stating that they were commanded "not to eat <u>or</u> to touch" the tree. She added to a simple command which was not too difficult to obey and this played a part in her deception and transgression of the commandment.

Mosheh specifically told Yisrael that the commandments were not too difficult. "[11] <u>*For this commandment which I command you this day is not too difficult for you, nor is it far off.*</u> [12] *It is not [a secret laid up] in heaven, that you should say, Who shall go up for us to heaven and bring it to us, that we may hear and do it?* [13] *Neither is it beyond the sea, that you should say, Who shall go over the sea for us and bring it to us, that we may hear and do it?* [14] *But the word is very near you, in your mouth and in your mind and in your heart, so that you can do it.*" Devarim 30:11-14 The Amplified Bible.

The Messianic Scriptures also confirm the fact that the commandments are not to difficult. "*For this is the love of Elohim, that we keep His commandments.* <u>*And His commandments are not burdensome.*</u>" 1 Yahanan 5:3.

These Scripture passages fly in the face of a common belief in Christianity that "we cannot keep the Law." There was a law which was oppressive and too difficult to bear - the laws and traditions of the religious leaders. The Apostle Kepha,[21] commonly called Peter, stated it clearly when he spoke to the Council at Jerusalem (Yahrushalayim)[22] which met to discuss the influx of

Gentile converts into the Community of Believers. He stated in Acts 15:10: "*why do you test Elohim by putting a yoke on the neck of the disciples which neither our fathers nor we were able to bear?*"

Many interpret this passage as if Kepha was stating that the new converts were not subject to the Torah, which was a burden that no one could obey. Nothing could be further from the truth. Kepha was speaking consistent with the ministry of the Messiah but his words are often misunderstood because people do not understand the ministry of the Messiah.

Messiah Yahushua spent much of His ministry distinguishing between the burdensome laws of men as opposed to the Torah. Before we look at the ministry of the Messiah though we must first set the stage for the religious environment into which He appeared and ministered approximately 2,000 years ago.

3

The Pharisees and the Law

In order to properly understand the Messianic Scriptures which detail the life and ministry of Yahushua, it is important to understand the religious and political climate in which He taught as well as the times when those texts were written.

During the ministry of Messiah, the Romans were in control of the Land of Yisrael. While the Romans were renowned for their fierce armies and their ruthlessness in dealing with aggressors, they continued a similar philosophy as that of the Greeks concerning their conquered territories. As much as possible they would allow their subjects to continue their cultural identities, when it did not conflict with the interests of Rome.

The Romans continued the Hellenistic traditions promoted and advanced by Alexander the Great and the successor dynasties resulting from the wars of the Diadochi. These societies contained a blending of many cultures and religions. They were polytheistic and pagan and thus believed in the existence of many different gods and goddesses. As a result, the faith of Yisrael, which worshipped only one

Elohim, was seen as strange and even repulsive. In fact, those that followed Elohim were often termed "atheists" because they did not believe in the popular gods.

Despite these differences, the Yisraelites were generally permitted to continue their religious observances including the operation of the Temple and the observance of the Scriptural Feasts found in Vayiqra (Leviticus) Chapter 23.[23]

The Yisraelites, while being a conquered people, were also a divided people. The Sadducees, the Pharisees, the Essenes and the Zealots were the primary sects of Yisraelites although they were by no means the only ones.[24] Without getting too deep into the doctrinal differences between the sects, the two most often referred to in the Messianic Scriptures were the Sadducees and the Pharisees. The Sadducees saw themselves as the physical and spiritual descendants of Zadok - a high priest of the family of Aaron. During the ministry of Yahushua they presided over the rites and the sacrifices of the Temple and made up most of the members of the Sanhedrin – the ruling body of Yisrael. They tended to be conservative, wealthy aristocrats and thus were elevated above the common man.

The Pharisees, on the other hand, tended to be middle class and were the primary contenders of the Sadducees. They were very much interested and involved in the daily application of the Torah in the lives of individual Yisraelites. Thus they were much more involved with the common man which was likely a significant factor in their prominence.

One of the primary differences between the two sects was their view of the Torah. The Pharisees believed

not only in the written Torah, but also the oral Torah which supposedly supplemented the written Torah. This gave way to the Pharisees being able to provide interpretations of the Torah which empowered them as they added their own customs, rules, regulations and laws to the instructions found in the written Torah.

According to the First Century Historian Flavius Josephus: "The Pharisees have delivered to the people a great many observances by succession from their fathers, which are not written in the laws of Moses; and for that reason it is that the Sadducees reject them, and say that we are to esteem those observances to be obligatory which are in the written word, but are not to observe what are derived from the tradition of our forefathers."[25]

The so called oral Torah has now been written down and is located primarily in the Talmud which includes the Mishnah and Gemara - there are also writings known as the Midrash. By calling the man made precepts the **oral Torah,** it gives them an immediate sense of credibility while, for the most part, the oral Torah is full of opinions, man made laws, customs and traditions which in many cases are an attempt to place a fence around the Torah.

The notion of erecting a fence around the Torah is a tradition developed by Judaism which sounds very pious at first until you see what is actually happening. To insure that people do not get close enough to the commandments to violate them – they put a fence in between men and the Torah. This keeps people far away from the Torah thus insuring that they do not disobey the Torah, but it often times obscures the real Torah and hides it behind

the commandments of men. The problem with the oral Torah and building a fence around the Torah is the fact that neither is supported by the Scriptures.

According to Shemot (Exodus) 24:3: ***"Mosheh came and told the people ALL the words of YHWH and ALL the judgments."*** In Shemot 24:4 the Scriptures also specifically state that "*Mosheh* ***wrote ALL of the Words of YHWH.***" Therefore, according to the clear reading of the Scriptures, I believe that Mosheh wrote ALL of the words. The only oral Torah that I subscribe to was the one transmitted to men before it was written by Mosheh which should in no way conflict with the Torah of Mosheh because they were the same.

The development of the oral Torah is quite significant because it provided the Pharisees with power over men. When any religious system or denomination is able to develop rules that dictate the lives and actions of its participants - those who make the rules thereby become empowered. The Torah specifically commands that: "*You shall not add to the word which I command you, nor take from it, that you may keep (shamar) the commandments of YHWH your Elohim which I command you.*" Devarim 4:3. The development of an oral Torah is a direct violation of this command because the oral laws often add to, subtract from or contradict the written Torah which results in a failure to keep the commandments.

Again, the word "keep" is shamar in Hebrew which is the same command given to Adam in the garden.

As discussed in the previous chapter the woman, Hawah, added to the Torah and literally, by adding the command "not to touch the tree," she in effect built her own fence around the Torah. Despite this vivid example men repeated her mistake by developing the oral Torah.

The laws and traditions which constitute the oral Torah are specifically known as the takanot (תקנות) and ma'asim (מעשים). The word takanot means "enactments" and refers to the laws enacted by the Pharisees. Ma'asim literally means "works or deeds" and refers to the precedents of the Rabbis that provide the source for Pharisaic rulings along with subsequent rulings based on those precedents.[26]

Over the centuries, these enactments and precedents developed into a powerful set of rules and regulations that have operated to define and control the religion now known as Judaism, which is quite different from the faith of ancient Yisrael. These enactments and precedents established by the Rabbis, the successors of the Pharisees, were given the same, if not greater weight, than the Torah.[27]

Read what the 12th Century Babylonian Sage Maimonides, also known as Rambam, wrote concerning this issue: "If there are 1000 prophets, all of them of the stature of Elijah and Elisha, giving a certain interpretation, and 1001 rabbis giving the opposite interpretation, you shall 'incline after the majority' (Shemot 23:2) and the law is according to the 1001 rabbis, not according to the 1000 venerable prophets. And thus our Sages said, 'By God, if we heard the matter directly from the mouth of Joshua the son of Nun, we would not obey him nor would we listen to him!' . . . And so if a prophet testifies that the Holy-One, Blessed be He, told him that the law of a certain

commandment is such and such, or [even] that the reasoning of a certain sage is correct, that prophet must be executed . . . as it is written, 'it is not in heaven' (Devarim 30:12). Thus God did not permit us to learn from the prophets, only from the Rabbis who are men of logic and reason."[28]

In my opinion, Rambam "destroyed the Torah" through this interpretation. In Torah study it was common to refer to a bad interpretation as "destroying the Torah" while a good interpretation would "fulfill the Torah." Rambam misquoted Scripture in an effort to derive from it what he wanted – an excuse to solidify the power of the Rabbis. Rambam used this reasoning to justify the execution of any prophet who prophesied that the Rabbis are wrong on any point of interpretation.

This was the same attitude that pervaded Pharisaic thought during the time of Yahushua which led to the execution of The Prophet – Messiah, and it was this very same spirit that Yahushua was confronting - men and their rules fighting against YHWH and His Torah. Just as their forefathers killed the Prophets (Luke 11:48) who confronted them and their errors, so too they killed Yahushua because He challenged their self imposed authority. This is at the core of most man-made religious systems - men fighting against their Creator and taking for themselves power, authority and glory which belongs to Him alone.

4

Messiah and the Torah

While the Pharisees were building their own kingdom, Yahushua came proclaiming the Kingdom of YHWH (Mark 1:14-15) and the Torah is the "constitution" of that Kingdom. He preached repentance which is the act of turning away from sin and back to the instructions of the Almighty – the Torah.

A wonderful Messianic prophesy provided in the Sefer Tehillim (Psalms) reads as follows: "[7] . . . *Behold, I come; in the volume of the scroll it is written of Me.* [8] *I delight to do Your will, O my Elohim, and* <u>*Your Torah is within My heart*</u>. [9] *I have proclaimed the good news of righteousness in the great assembly; Indeed, I do not restrain my lips, O YHWH, You Yourself know.* [10] *I have not hidden Your righteousness within My heart; I have declared Your faithfulness and Your salvation; I have not concealed Your lovingkindness and Your truth from the great assembly.*" Tehillim 40:7-10.

This text reveals that the Torah would be in the heart of the Messiah and it is all about Him. The passage proclaims "*I come in the volume (roll) of the scroll it is written of Me.*" In other words, the Torah should point to the Messiah and everything He said and did should be consistent with the Torah.

Interestingly, the final words of the Tanak in most English Bibles come from the Prophet Malachi which reads: "[4] ***Remember the Torah of Mosheh,*** *My servant, which I commanded him in Horeb for all Yisrael, with the statutes and judgments.* [5] *Behold, I will send you Elijah the prophet before the coming of the great and dreadful day of YHWH.* [6] *And he will turn the hearts of the fathers to the children, and the hearts of the children to their fathers, lest I come and strike the earth with a curse.*" Malachi 4:4-6.

Messiah stated that John the Baptist, more accurately known as Yahanan the Immerser, was Elijah (Eliyahu) who came to "*Prepare the way of YHWH; make straight His paths.*" This is a direct reference to the Torah. Yahanan preached "*Repent for the Kingdom of Heaven is at hand.*" (Mattityahu 3:2). This is also the same thing that Yahushua preached when He began His ministry: "*Repent for the Kingdom of Heaven is at hand.*" (Mattityahu 4:17). A close examination of His ministry reveals that everything that He taught was about the Kingdom and the Torah, which contains the rules of the Kingdom.

So there was no mistake regarding His position on the Torah, Yahushua made a very clear and unequivocal statement during one of His first public teachings commonly called "The Sermon on the Mount." He specifically stated: "[17] *Do not think that I came to destroy the Torah or the Prophets. I did not come to destroy but to fulfill.* [18] *For assuredly, I say to you, till heaven and earth pass away, one jot or one tittle will by no means pass from the Torah till all is fulfilled.* [19] ***Whoever therefore breaks one of the least of these commandments, and teaches men so, shall be called least in the Kingdom of Heaven; but whoever does and teaches them, he shall be called great in the Kingdom of Heaven.***" Mattithyahu

5:17-19. There are Hebrew versions of Mattityahu which read a little different but make the point even stronger. Some have the Messiah stating: "*Do not think that I came to add to or subtract from the Torah.*"

Christians often struggle with this passage because it does not synchronize with their understanding of the Law and grace. The popular Christian mantra that "we are under grace and not under the Law" has been useful in justifying the notion that Christians do not have to obey the instructions of YHWH found in the Torah, despite the fact that a contextual examination of the Scriptures clearly reveals otherwise.

One of the reasons for the confusion surrounding Yahushua's statement is that people often think of "fulfilling" as completing or bringing something to an end. What Yahushua meant was that He came "to make perfect" or "to fill up, to give meaning" and to show the heart of the Torah. In essence, the Pre-Messianic Scriptures found in the Tanak were incomplete without the Messiah. Thus He did not come to do away with the Torah, but rather to fill it up with meaning. He showed us what it was really like to live and walk according to the instructions of YHWH – He became our living, breathing example – the Word became flesh.

David H. Stern in his commentary on Mattityahu 5:17 states: "[t]he Greek word for 'to complete' is 'plerosai,' literally, 'to fill;' the usual rendering here, however, is 'to fulfill.' Replacement theology, which wrongly teaches that the Church has replaced the Jews as [Elohim's] people, understands this verse wrongly . . . [Yahushua's] 'fulfilling' the Torah is thought to mean that it is unnecessary for people to fulfill it now. But there is no logic to the presupposition that [Yahushua's] obeying the Torah does away with our need to obey it . . . [Yahushua] did not come to abolish but 'to make full' (plerosai) the meaning of what the Torah and the ethical demands of the Prophets require. Thus He came to complete our understanding of the Torah and the Prophets so that we can try more effectively to be and do what they say to be and do."[29]

Mr. Stern is quite correct when he links Replacement Theology with the teaching that Yahushua's fulfillment of the Torah resulted in the abolition of the Torah. The text very clearly and succinctly says the exact opposite. Only when you try to apply a preconceived theology that the "Church" has replaced Yisrael and that grace has replaced the Torah would you ever even attempt to construe the text in such a fashion.

It is important to note that twice in verse 17 Yahushua states that He *did not come to destroy the Torah*. He then goes on to state the converse - that He came to fill up or fulfill the Torah - these are clearly different objectives. Destroy means to do away with and He specifically said that He did not come to do that. The word plerosai (πληρωσαι) which is often translated as "fulfill" in that particular passage does not, and cannot, mean to do away with, otherwise Yahushua would be contradicting Himself. Therefore when Yahushua said that He came to fulfill the Torah He did not mean that He came to do away with the Torah.

Further, when Yahushua said that "*till heaven and earth pass away not one jot or one tittle*" of the Torah would pass away, He was making a very precise and definitive statement. First of all He gave a time frame, which is the passing of heaven and earth. Since heaven and earth are

still here, it is very safe to say that the Torah has not passed away. Second, He said that not one jot or tittle would pass from the Torah till **all** is fulfilled.

It is commonly taught that the jot is meant to signify the "iota" (ι) and the "yud" (י) which are the smallest letters in the Greek and Hebrew alphabets and a tittle, which is a stroke, a dot or other marking made on the Torah scroll such as the decorative spurs added to Hebrew characters. This is certainly an accurate understanding, but there is another interpretation regarding the jots and the tittles which is a little more profound.

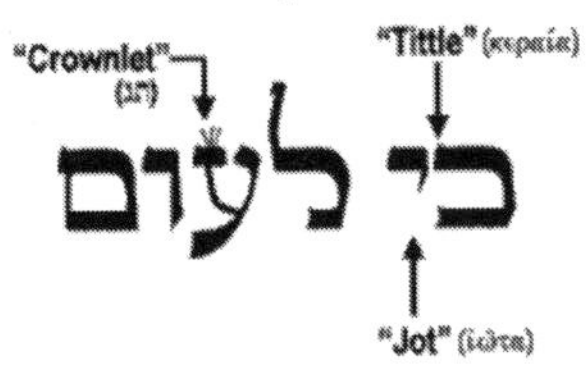

Aside from the observable Hebrew characters written on a Torah Scroll, there are other messages imbedded within the text which are not discernable unless you examine a Hebrew Scroll. The reason is because there are many un-translated markings which were allegedly written by Mosheh and included in every Torah Scroll written thereafter. These are not necessarily as apparent as the "jots" and "tittles" and could easily be missed by the casual reader. These markings include such things as dots, enlarged letters, reduced letters, inverted letters, reversed letters, elongated letters and gaps, all with special meaning, but none of them are ever translated. Therefore, if you only review an English translation of the Torah you will never even see these things. Thus, the jots and the tittles can be interpreted to mean, not only the Hebrew characters and the strokes and spurs added to them, but also the dots and the

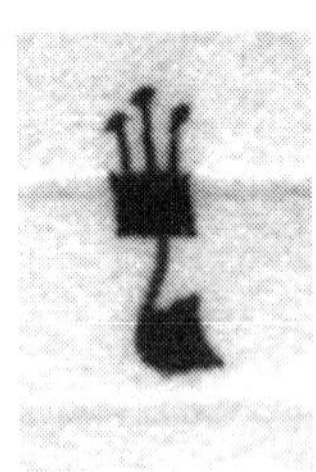

markings which are not even translated such as the inverted nun depicted above.

With either interpretation, the resounding point being made is that nothing in the Torah, not even the smallest mark or letter – whether translated or not - will change or pass away as long as heaven and earth are still in existence. This seems profound and is certainly contrary to accepted Christian theology, even though it was spoken by the Messiah at the beginning of the Messianic Scriptures. Only when you fully comprehend this important statement can you then understand the teachings of the Messiah in their proper context - as well as His famous confrontations with the Scribes and the Pharisees.

5

Messiah and the Pharisees

Once it is understood that Yahushua affirmed the Torah and its' continuing validity "***until all is fulfilled and as long as Heaven and Earth remain***" we can then begin to see that all of His teachings were in absolute agreement with the Torah. The reason that He made this proclamation was because the religious leaders had added to, and subtracted from the Torah through their takanot and ma'asim. Yahushua came to restore the Torah to the people and part of this mission involved confronting the self-imposed authority of the Pharisees.

The Pharisees believed that they had the authority to interpret the Torah and to instruct people how to obey the Torah. It is important to recognize that the Torah gave no such authority to rabbis, only the priests, prophets and kings had spiritual authority in Yisrael. Yahushua came to challenge the rabbinic authority and this was the underlying controversy concerning most, if not all, of their confrontations.

At times we read about the Messiah doing some rather peculiar things which do not necessarily make sense because we do not always understand this underlying conflict. As part of His ministry He confronted the

religious leadership and intentionally violated their man-made laws. By doing so He was knocking down the fence that they had build around the Torah.

For instance, His first recorded miracle of turning water into wine was a direct affront to their tradition concerning ceremonially purified water. For those familiar with the mikvah[30] it is clear why people would have large quantities of water for ritual immersions in their home, although it is questionable whether an immersion pool in a home actually qualifies as living water. Since most people used liquid containers to store either wine or water, it would have been important to thoroughly wash the containers to remove any remnant of wine if they were going to hold ritually purified water.

According to tradition, this water was not to have any vinegar taste or evidence of wine, otherwise it would not be considered pure. By using these designated water jugs which were filled with water that was then turned into wine, Yahushua was sending a powerful message concerning their customs. (Yahanan 2:6).[31]

On another occasion, using saliva, Yahushua made clay and placed it into a man's eyes to heal him which was in direct contradiction to the man-made laws regarding what could be done on the Sabbath. According to tradition, it was a violation to make anything on the Sabbath and, believe it or not, it was prohibited to put saliva in a person's eyes to heal them on the Sabbath.[32] There were also those who considered it a violation to heal on the Sabbath. Therefore in this one instance He violated three of the man-made laws but none of the Torah commandments. (Yahanan 9:1).

Yahushua provided another wonderful example of breaking the laws of men when he healed the man with the withered hand on the Sabbath. (Mattityahu 12:9-13). According to the Pharisees, such conduct was not permitted on the Sabbath. This, of course, is absurd because nowhere in the Torah does it ever put any prohibitions on healing, especially on the Sabbath. There are very few commandments concerning the Sabbath in the Torah but the Pharisees had developed hundreds. Again, it is apparent that Yahushua calculated His actions to challenge the authority of the Pharisees and their takanot although He always observed the Torah.

In fact, in another instance of healing, Yahushua specifically instructed the leper to obey the Torah after he had been healed. "[12] *And it happened when He was in a certain city, that behold, a man who was full of leprosy saw Yahushua; and he fell on his face and implored Him, saying, 'Master, if You are willing, You can make me clean.'* [13] *Then He put out His hand and touched him, saying, 'I am willing; be cleansed.' Immediately the leprosy left him.*[14] *And He charged him to tell no one, '<u>But go and show yourself to the priest, and make an offering for your cleansing, as a testimony to them, just as Mosheh commanded.</u>'*" Luke 5:12-14.

In this case, the man recognized he was diseased and unclean, just as we need to recognize that our transgressions make us unclean. He had faith that Yahushua could heal him and, in fact, Yahushua demonstrated that He was willing to heal him. The man was touched by Yahushua and he was healed. The fact that Yahushua touched a leper was quite incredible because generally people would avoid lepers as being tamei (טמא). In fact, a leper was required to tear their clothing, shave their head and cry

out "Unclean! Unclean!" so that people would not go near them. (Vayiqra 13:45-46). Instead of avoiding the leper, Yahushua touched him – what a wonderful demonstration of His love and compassion. He then instructed the man to obey the Torah concerning the healing of leprosy which is found in Vayiqra 4:1-32.[33]

This particular mitzvot[34] is very detailed and I suspect was not done very often, if ever. Notice that Yahushua instructed the man to obey the Torah "*as a testimony to them*" - meaning the priests. This is usually the case with our obedience to the Torah - it is for our blessing, but it is also a testimony to others. Surely this must have amazed the priests to see a man healed from leprosy for this was a well understood and accepted sign of the Messiah.

Yahushua clearly instructed people to obey the Torah and I believe He often instructed His disciples and others to disobey the takanot intentionally so that He could point out the error of the Pharisees. A good example of this fact is when the disciples were walking through grain fields on the Sabbath (Luke 6:1-2). As they walked they plucked heads of grain, rubbed them in their hands and ate them. Seeing this, some of the Pharisees asked Yahushua why they were doing something which was not permitted on the Sabbath.[35] Again, you can search the Torah high and low and you will not find any commandment prohibiting such conduct on the Sabbath although it was prohibited by the traditions of men.

In another instance of healing Yahushua told a paralyzed man waiting by the pool at the

Sheep Gate called Beit Zatha: "[8] . . . *'Rise, take up your bed and walk.'* [9] *And immediately the man was made well, took up his bed, and walked. And that day was the Sabbath.* [10] *The Yahudim therefore said to him who was cured, 'It is the Sabbath; it is not lawful for you to carry your bed.'"* Yahanan 5:8-10. The word bed most likely refers to a mattress or a mat and instead of focusing on the miraculous healing the religious men criticized the man for carrying his mat - a violation of their takanot.

In my opinion, there is no other passage of Scripture that more succinctly demonstrates the focus of Yahushua's teaching than on the issue of washing of the hands. First read the account and then I will elaborate.

"[1] *Then the Scribes and Pharisees who were from Yahrushalayim came to Yahushua, saying,* [2] *'Why do Your disciples transgress the tradition of the elders? For they do not wash their hands when they eat bread.'* [3] *He answered and said to them, 'Why do you also transgress the commandment of Elohim because of your tradition?'* [4] *For Elohim commanded, saying, 'Honor your father and your mother' and, 'He who curses father or mother, let him be put to death.'* [5] *But you say, 'Whoever says to his father or mother, 'Whatever profit you might have received from me is a gift to Elohim'* - [6] *then he need not honor his father or mother.' Thus you have made the commandment of Elohim of no effect by your tradition.* [7] *Hypocrites! Well did Yeshayahu (Isaiah) prophesy about you, saying:* [8] *'These people draw near to Me with their mouth, and honor Me with their lips, but their heart is far from Me.* [9] *And in vain they worship Me, teaching as doctrines the commandments of men.'"* Mattityahu 15:1-9.

To fully understand what is going on in this text it is helpful to understand the historical background as well as

to go beyond the English text. As discussed, the Pharisees had developed their own religious traditions apart from the Torah, one of them being the commandment concerning the washing of the hands. While many who read this passage believe that there is actually a commandment concerning the washing of hands in the Torah - they are mistaken. This is really nothing more than a man-made tradition – you will not find this commandment anywhere in the Torah.

Regardless, the tradition exists to this day known as Netilat Yadaim. The following is a sample liturgy commonly used by those in Judaism to fulfill their inherited takanot. This one is done before making bread.

<u>Washing the Hands for Challah</u>

- Make sure your hands are clean and dry.
- Grasp the washing cup with your right hand.
- Transfer the washing cup to your left hand.
- Make a loose fist of your right hand.
- Pour water over your right hand -- enough to wet both the inside and outside of your right fist.
- Repeat.
- Transfer the washing cup to your right hand.
- Pour water over your left hand -- enough to wet both the inside and outside of your left fist.
- Repeat.
- Loosely cup your hands, palms upwards, as if to "accept" the purity, raise your hands and recite:

  Ba-rooch Attah A-doy-noy,
  E-lo-hay-noo Melech ha-olam,
  asher ki-di-sha-noo bi-mi-tz-vo-sav,
  vi-tzee-va-noo al ni-tee-las ya-da-yim.

  (Blessed are You Hashem (the Master) our G-d (Source of our strength) Ruler of the universe, Who has made us holy (special to Him) through His commandments, and commanded us concerning washing (our) hands.)

  Dry your hands perfectly.[36]

While the Pharisees may not have followed this exact procedure, this is the end result of the takanot which they were referencing. Notice that in their prayer they state that YHWH commanded us concerning washing our hands - which He did not. While it is certainly not a bad idea to wash your hands before you eat, it is not a commandment.

If you examine the Hebrew text of Mattityahu the essence of the conflict is crystal clear. The Pharisees first confront Yahushua by asking Him: "*Why do your disciples (talmidim) transgress the takanot of antiquity by not washing their hands before eating?*" Amazingly, they considered it a transgression to disobey a takanot. Yahushua responded to them by asking: "*Why do you transgress the Words of Elohim because of your takanot?*" Notice He calls it <u>their</u> takanot which is absolutely correct. It is not in the Torah and the takanot is not from YHWH - it is from men.

Yahushua was giving the religious elite a lesson in the Torah. He was also rebuking them for placing their own traditions above the Torah and, in fact, replacing the Torah and making it of no effect. A remarkable aspect of this passage is that Yahushua quotes the Prophet Yeshayahu (Isaiah) during part of the rebuke which goes to show that the conduct of the Pharisees was nothing new - it had been prophesied hundreds of years in advance.

I have provided just a small number of examples which clearly demonstrate the motivation behind much of Yahushua's conduct. His actions were often a direct affront to the takanot of the religious leaders and unless you understand the dynamics of what was going on you will miss much of the flavor of His ministry. Armed with this insight, it is my hope that the reader can now study the

Messianic Scriptures in a new light and see that Yahushua kept His word. He did not come to add to or take away from the Torah but to show us the fullness of the Torah.

The religious leaders had hidden the Torah from most people and Yahushua came to reveal the Torah and expose the Pharisees - He was right in their face. In Mattityahu 23:27-28 we read as Messiah proclaims: "[27] *Woe to you, Scribes and Pharisees, hypocrites! For you are like whitewashed tombs which indeed appear beautiful outwardly, but inside are full of dead men's bones and all uncleanness.* [28] *Even so you also* ***outwardly appear righteous to men, but inside you are full of hypocrisy and lawlessness.***"

The word lawlessness comes from the Greek word anomias (ανομιασ) which specifically means: "**without Torah.**" Therefore, the very people who were supposed to be teaching the Torah are accused of not having the Torah in them. Through their takanot and ma'asim they **added to** and **took away** from the Torah. They placed heavy burdens upon men which was the exact opposite of what the Torah was intended to do. The Torah was given to a redeemed people who were former slaves. It was not intended to put them back into bondage - it was meant for a free people. This is why Yahushua specifically stated that His yoke - which is the Torah - is light and easy. (Mattityahu 11:30).[37]

One of the reasons why the Pharisees sought to kill Yahushua was because He challenged their authority and the issue of authority continued after the death and resurrection of Messiah and eventually permeated the Assembly of Believers. Shaul even felt the need to clarify the matter of authority when he addressed the Corinthian assembly: "*But I want you to know that the head of every man*

is Messiah, the head of woman is man, and the head of Messiah is Elohim." 1 Corinthians 11:3. Notice that there are no popes, bishops, rabbis, priests, pastors or elders mentioned here. The family unit is the most important structure created by YHWH and spiritual authority flows from Elohim through the family unit.

Sadly, religious oligarchs continue to place themselves between men and YHWH and between husbands and their wives and children. It seems that almost every religious system has its own hierarchy and power structure which places the masses, also known as the laity, at the bottom of the power pyramid. This is where we get the term Nicolaitan. Two Greek root words "nico" and "laos" are brought together to form "nicolaitan." Nico means "to conquer or bind" while Laos means "the common people." This notion of conquering or ruling over the common people is what Yahushua called the doctrine of the Nicolaitans and it was the only thing that I am aware of that He said He hated. (Revelation 2:6 and 2:15).[38]

Rabbinic Judaism was spawned from Pharisaism and continues to teach that the Rabbis have the authority to interpret the Torah. I am dismayed by the fact that there are many in the modern Messianic movement who claim to follow Yahushua but at the same time subscribe to this teaching. As a result, they are placing themselves under the spiritual authority of a religious system which not only denies the fact that Yahushua was the Messiah but also has a history of profaning the Name and ministry of Yahushua and actively works against Believers through the efforts of those called "Anti-missionaries."[39]

Yahushua said: "[49] *For I have not spoken on My own authority; but the Father who sent Me gave Me a command, what I should say and what I should speak.*[50] ***And I know that His command is everlasting life. Therefore, whatever I speak, just as the Father has told Me, so I speak.*** " Yahanan 12:49-50 NKJV. It is clear that what Yahushua speaks is from the Father and He says that His command is everlasting life. He is the head of every man, not the Pope, a Priest or Pastor nor the Pharisees or their successors, the Rabbis. That is the bottom line on religious authority.

Interestingly, Yahushua seems to contradict this fact by instructing His followers to obey the Pharisees in one passage found in the Good News according to Mattityahu. So what do we make of the following statement attributed to the Messiah from the New King James translation: "[2] *The Scribes and the Pharisees sit in Moses' seat.* [3] *Therefore whatever they tell you to observe, that observe and do, but do not do according to their works; for they say, and do not do.* [4] *For they bind heavy burdens, hard to bear, and lay them on men's shoulders; but they themselves will not move them with one of their fingers.*" Mattityahu 23:2-5 NKJV.

This version seems to conflict with other teachings of Yahushua when He consistently corrects the Scribes and Pharisees and challenges their authority. In this passage He seems to be telling people to follow the Scribes and the Pharisees by doing what they tell people to do but not follow their example in how they act. If this was actually what He was teaching then He would indeed be contradicting Himself. The reason for the confusion is because most modern versions of the scriptures mistranslate this passage.

A proper rendering of this passage should read as follows: "[2] *The Scribes and the Pharisees sit in Mosheh's seat.*

[3] *Therefore whatever he [Mosheh] tells you to observe, that observe and do, but do not do according to their works; for they say, and do not do.* [4] *For they bind heavy burdens, hard to bear, and lay them on men's shoulders; but they themselves will not move them with one of their fingers.* [5] *But all their works they do to be seen by men. They widen their tefillin and enlarge the tzitzit of their garments.* [6] *They love the best places at feasts, the best seats in the synagogues,* [7] *greetings in the marketplaces, and to be called by men, 'Rabbi.'"* Mattityahu 23:2-8.[40]

This passage is translated from the Aramaic and Hebrew texts of Mattityahu[41] and clearly sets forth the intention of Yahushua. The seat of Mosheh is a chair found in some ancient synagogues and it is believed that this would be the place where the person would sit that read the Torah or where the Torah Scroll would be placed when not in use.[42]

The meaning of the phrase "*the Scribes and the Pharisees sit in Mosheh's seat*" is not absolutely clear as it could be both literal and metaphorical. Some believe that Yahushua was recognizing their authority but it could simply mean that they were the ones who kept charge of the Torah scrolls which were quite rare and valuable. One thing that is clear is the fact that Yahushua was telling people to do what Mosheh says, not what the Pharisees do. In other words, what Mosheh said and what the Pharisees did was not always the same, therefore defer to Mosheh and do what he instructed.

Yahushua also made an interesting comment which is often overlooked. He stated in verse 5: "*But their works they do to be seen by men. They make broad straps for their teffilin and enlarge the tzitzit of their mantles.*" This statement will seem quite foreign for anyone unfamiliar with the commandments concerning teffilin and tzitzit.

Teffilin, also called phylacteries, are worn to fulfill the commandments found in Shemot 13:9, Devarim 6:8 as well as Devarim 11:18 which provide direction concerning the instructions to "*bind them as a sign on your hand, and they shall be as frontlets between your eyes.*" The Pharisees, instead of wearing modest teffilin wore large teffilin to impress men.

Likewise, the tzitzit (ציצית), often called tassels or fringes, are commanded in the Torah in two separate instances. In Devarim 22:12 YHWH commands: "*Make tzitzit on the four corners of the garment with which you cover yourself.*" According to Bemidbar (Numbers) 15:37-41: "[37] *YHWH spoke to Mosheh, saying,* [38] *Speak to the children of Yisrael, and you shall say to them to make tzitziyot on the corners of their garments throughout their generations, and to put a blue cord in the tzitzit of the corners.* [39] *And it shall be to you for a tzitzit, and you shall see it, and shall remember all the commands of YHWH and shall do them, and not search after your own heart and your own eyes after which you went whoring,* [40] *so that you remember, and shall do all my commands, and be set apart unto your Elohim.* [41] *I am YHWH your Elohim, who brought you out of the land of Mitsrayim (Egypt), to be your Elohim. I am YHWH your Elohim.*"

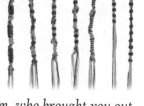

They did not just wear simple tefillin, they wore

very large ones. They did not just wear tzitzit, they wore *very long* tzitzit as if the size of their tefillin or tzitzit demonstrated their degree of piousness. Their obedience became a show and was mere pageantry which was not the result intended by the very commandments which they were supposed to be obeying. The tzitzit and the tefillin are intended to remind us of the commandments so that we walk in obedience but the Pharisees were turning these reminders into religious badges which was in complete contradiction with their intended purpose.

Their hearts were not right and their intentions were misplaced. The point here is that Yahushua was not criticizing the fact that they obeyed the Torah but rather the manner in which they obeyed. Clearly Yahushua Himself obeyed the commandments and we can see an incredible fulfillment of prophesy in and through His Torah observance.

A prophecy in the Tanak speaks of the Messiah as follows: "*The Sun of Righteousness shall arise with healing in His wings.*" Malachi 4:2 NKJV. These "wings" are kanaph (כּנף) in Hebrew and refer to the edge of a garment, which is the tzitzit. We read in the Good News according to Luke: "[43] *Now a woman, having a flow of blood for twelve years, who had spent all her livelihood on physicians and could not be healed by any,* [44] *came from behind and touched the border of His garment. And immediately her flow of blood stopped.*" Luke 8:43-44 NKJV. The Greek word used to describe a border is kraspedon (κρασπεδον) which means a fringe or tassel. In other words, she grabbed His tzitzit which He was wearing in obedience to the Torah and He came with healing in His tzitzit just as was foretold by the Prophet Malachi.

Also, in Mattithyahu 14:35-36 we read: "[35] *And when the men of that place (Gennesar) recognized Him, they sent out into all that surrounding country, and brought to Him all who were sick,* [36] *and begged Him to let them only touch the tzitzit of His garment. And as many as touched it were completely healed.*"

We see in these passages not only a beautiful fulfillment of prophecy, but also an example of the Torah observance of Yahushua which has been obscured due to translation inconsistencies and ignorance on the part of translators. By grabbing hold of the tztizit - which represent the commandments, the terms of the Covenant - people were shown that healing and blessings come through the Torah which is what Messiah came to teach and fulfill.

6

Messiah Teaches Torah

A close examination of the Scriptures reveals many striking similarities between Yahushua and Mosheh[43] and this should be of no surprise since Mosheh provided a vivid description of the Messiah in the Sefer Devarim.[44]

"15 *YHWH your Elohim will raise up for you a Prophet like me from your midst, from your brethren. Him you shall hear,* 16 *according to all you desired of YHWH your Elohim in Horeb in the day of the assembly, saying, 'Let me not hear again the voice of YHWH my Elohim, nor let me see this great fire anymore, lest I die.'* 17 *And YHWH said to me: 'What they have spoken is good.* 18 *I will raise up for them a Prophet like you from among their brethren, and will put My words in His mouth, and He shall speak to them all that I command Him.* 19 *And it shall be that whoever will not hear My words, which He speaks in My Name, I will require it of him.'"* Devarim 18:15-19.

Those anticipating the Messiah would therefore be looking for someone "like Mosheh" - someone Who would speak in the Name of YHWH and follow His commands. One of the most significant roles of Mosheh was the fact that He was the mediator of the Covenant between YHWH and Yisrael. That Covenant was a continuation of the Covenant previously made with

Avraham. It was a marriage Covenant[45] between YHWH and Yisrael and because Yisrael the Bride sinned and broke the Covenant it needed to be renewed. The Messiah did not come to do away with the former Covenant and mediate a brand new Covenant, rather He came to restore and mediate the Renewed Covenant[46] prophesied by the Prophet Yirmeyahu (Jeremiah).[47]

Remember that YHWH only uttered the Ten Commandments to Yisrael. The people could not listen to the voice of YHWH and asked if Mosheh would meet with YHWH and relate His words to the assembly. Therefore, although the Torah was from YHWH, it came through Mosheh. Likewise with Yahushua, the Word made flesh, the Word of YHWH came through Him.

He was like Mosheh in that He instructed people concerning the Torah with authority - He was "The Prophet" foretold by Mosheh. He ascended the Mountain and taught Torah to the people just as Mosheh did yet often He is viewed as opposing or contradicting Mosheh. The general belief is that Mosheh taught "*eye for an eye*" and Yahushua taught "*turn the other cheek*" – Mosheh taught "*hate your enemy*" while Yahushua taught to "*love your enemy.*" We shall soon see that these seeming contradictions are not contradictions at all, nor are they necessarily accurate. It must be clearly understood that Yahushua was unambiguous about the fact that He and Mosheh agreed. He specifically stated: "[46] *For if you believed Mosheh, you would believe Me; for he wrote about Me.* [47] *But if you do not believe his writings, how will you believe My words?*" Yahanan 5:46-47.

We have discussed the fact that the Pharisees were asserting their authority to interpret the Torah of Mosheh

and Yahushua directly challenged that authority. He also clearly stated that He in no way intended on destroying the Torah and, until heaven and earth pass away, not the smallest part of the Torah will pass away. We also have seen that He taught people to do as Mosheh told them to do, not follow the Pharisees when they deviated from the Torah. With that understanding now we can properly view the teachings of the Messiah.

The Messianic Scriptures are, in large part, a commentary on the Torah and the Tanak. There is not enough room in this book to discuss all of the teachings of Yahushua in light of the Torah, suffice it to say that all of His teachings were about the Torah.

Some people believe that Yahushua changed the commandments or reduced them to just two. They use the following passage to support their position. "34 *But the Pharisees having heard that He had silenced the Sadducees, were gathered together,* 35 *and one of them, one learned in the Torah, did question, trying Him and saying* 36 *'Teacher, which is the greatest commandment in the Torah?'* 37 *Yahushua replied: 'Love YHWH your Elohim with all your heart and with all your soul and with all your mind.'* 38 *This is the first and greatest commandment.* 39 *And the second is like it: 'Love your neighbor as yourself.'* 40 *All the Torah and the Prophets hang on these two commandments.*" Mattithyahu 22:36-40 (see also Mark 12:29-31).

What most Christians do not realize is that this is pure Torah taught by the Word made flesh. Since Christians do not necessarily believe that the Torah applies to them, they often miss the fact that Yahushua quoted "The Shema"[48] which is arguably the most important prayer and Scripture to the people of Yisrael - "4 *Hear, O*

Yisrael: YHWH our Elohim, YHWH is One! [5] *You shall love YHWH your Elohim with all your heart, with all your soul, and with all your strength.*" Devarim 6:4-5 NKJV.

He also quoted Vayiqra 19:18: "*You shall not take vengeance, nor bear any grudge against the children of your people, but you shall love your neighbor as yourself: I am YHWH.*" As we can plainly see - He was teaching from the Torah. He did not say that these were the only commandments and that He was abolishing the rest - He simply revealed that love was at the very heart of the Torah and He showed us the priority of our love and relationships.

Yahushua revealed how the Pharisees confused things by imposing their traditions and customs which became a burden rather than a joy. They attempted to achieve righteousness through their man-made customs, traditions and laws and by doing so lost sight of the pure Torah. Yahushua was distinguishing between the traditions and laws of the Pharisees (takanot and ma'asim) and the unadulterated instructions of YHWH found in the Torah.

Still others quote passages such as Mattityahu 5:38-45 to prove that Yahushua changed the Torah. The portion reads as follows: "[38] *You have heard that it was said, 'An eye for an eye and a tooth for a tooth.'* [39] *But I tell you not to resist an evil person. But whoever slaps you on your right cheek, turn the other to him also.* [40] *If anyone wants to sue you and take away your tunic, let him have your cloak also.* [41] *And whoever compels you to go one mile, go with him two.* [42] *Give to him who asks you, and from him who wants to borrow from you do not turn away.* [43] *You have heard that it was said, 'You shall love your neighbor and hate your enemy.'* [44] *But I say to you, love your enemies, bless those who curse you, do good to those who*

hate you, and pray for those who spitefully use you and persecute you, [45] *that you may be sons of your Father in heaven; for He makes His sun rise on the evil and on the good, and sends rain on the just and on the unjust."* Mattityahu 5:38-45.

This is a greatly misunderstood passage because you must know and appreciate the Torah to comprehend the teaching. First of all, when Yahushua refers to "*an eye for an eye and a tooth for a tooth*" He is specifically referencing the Torah, in particular Shemot 21:20-27 which refers to the treatment of people who were considered the property of others.

The allusion that Yahushua is making concerns the maltreatment of a bondservant[49] which is detailed in Shemot 21:1-11. He is telling His disciples that if they belong to YHWH, then they look to Him for their justice and they do not need to pursue the justice of a freeman which seeks retribution or compensation. If we are bondservants then we look to our Master for justice.[50] Yahushua was not changing the Torah, rather He was teaching something that was always in the Torah. He was simply elaborating on the heart of the Torah and instructing His disciples to go beyond the letter of the Torah.

As an innocent and blameless man He did not deserve to be judged and mistreated by men - let alone killed. He had the right to seek justice for Himself, but He came as a bondservant (Yeshayahu 42) and in that capacity He did not seek His own will, but that of His Master.

With that understanding we then read Yahushua making a rather peculiar statement: *You have heard that it was said, 'You shall love your neighbor and hate your enemy.'* The problem with this passage is that the Torah never instructed anyone to hate their enemy. This begs the question: Did Yahushua misquote the Torah? That is not possible since He was the Torah in flesh. While this was not a direct quote from the Torah it was a common teaching of the Essene Sect.[51] The Torah always taught that an individual should show kindness to an enemy when the opportunity presented itself (Shemot 23:4-5) and Yahushua taught His disciples, as bondservants, they were to love their enemies and let their Master take care of the rest.

It is clear then that Yahushua was never changing, adding or taking away from the Torah - He was always explaining and revealing the depth of the Torah - the heart of the Torah or as He described them - "*the weightier matters of the Torah.*" Often times the religious leaders got so caught up in the minutia that they forgot what was really important.

This is evident to this day when you walk around the streets of Jerusalem and see all of the religious people wearing their religious accoutrements while at the same time barreling through crowds and being rude to one another without any semblance of peace, joy or love emanating from their beings. Now this is not to say that all religious people act this way because I have met many wonderful people who would be classified as religious. Sadly though, it is a common enough occurrence to warrant observation and give pause for concern.

Yahushua aptly demonstrated this point to the Pharisees in an account recorded in Mattityahu 23:23 as follows: "*Woe to you, Scribes and Pharisees, hypocrites! For you pay tithe of mint and anise and cummin, and have neglected the weightier matters of the Torah: justice and mercy and faith. These you ought to have done, without leaving the others undone.*"

To properly understand this statement it is important to understand the tithe. Christianity typically recognizes the tithe as a commandment even though it is in the Torah, which is a glaring contradiction in their theology. For the purposes of this discussion we will look at one of the primary passages in the Torah concerning the tithe found in Sefer Devarim. "[22] ***You shall truly tithe all the increase of your grain that the field produces year by year.*** [23] *And you shall eat before YHWH your Elohom, in the place where He chooses to make His Name abide,* ***the tithe of your grain and your new wine and your oil, of the firstborn of your herds and your flocks,*** *that you may learn to fear YHWH your Elohim always.*" Devarim 14:22-23.

The tithe revolved around the Scriptural Appointed Times described in Vayiqra 23 which are intimately connected to the major harvests in the Land. The object was that after the harvest, people would bring their offerings up to the place where YHWH designated and enjoy a celebration. For a long time it was located at Shiloh and later, under the reign of King David, it was moved to Yahrushalayim. When Yisrael obeyed, it was a demonstration of the blessings promised within the Torah.

The tithe was on the increase and the Scriptures refer to the first fruits of grain, grapes, olives and flocks. There is no mention of herbs or the need to tithe herbs although if you want to, you are free to tithe them. In fact, if you grow some herbs in your little herb garden at home

and then harvest those herbs it is a great thing to honor YHWH and give Him the first fruits.

The point that Yahushua was making was that they did things which were not even specifically prescribed in the Torah - yet at the same time – they missed the most important things that they were supposed to learn: justice, mercy and faith. In a similar passage in Luke 11:42 it refers to "*justice and the love of Elohim.*" These are the important lessons that we are supposed to be learning through the Torah and these are the things that Yahushua came to teach us.

With that understanding we can look to other teachings and see how He was showing us the depth of the commandments. "[21]*Have you not heard what was said to those of old: 'You shall not murder and whoever murders is guilty of a judgment of death?'* [22] *But I say to you, he who angers his companion is guilty of judgment; he who calls his brother inferior shall be guilty of judgment before the congregation; (he) who calls him a fool is guilty of the fire of Gehenna.*" Mattithyahu 5:21-22. Wait a minute - He is telling us not only to obey the letter of the Torah, but the Spirit of the Torah. In other words, He is concerned with matters of the heart, not just outward acts and appearances.

He taught in a similar fashion concerning another commandment. "[27] *You have heard that it was said, 'Do not commit adultery.'* [28] *But I tell you that anyone who looks at a woman lustfully has already committed adultery with her in his heart.*" Mattityahu 5:27-28 NIV. There He goes again! He is expecting more than the written Torah requires - He is talking about our hearts. Of course this is what Mosheh instructed (Devarim 10:16; 30:6) and it was prophesied concerning the Renewed Covenant – that our hearts would

be circumcised. (Ezekiel 36:22-38; see also Ezekiel 44:6-9).

Yahushua was distinguishing between obedience from the heart and external obedience for the benefit of men. He desires obedience from the heart, not just superficial observances. This is why he told the Pharisees to: "*first cleanse the inside of the cup and dish, that the outside of them may be clean also.*" Mattityahu 23:26. They were more concerned with obeying the "letter of the law" to prove their righteousness externally, for the sake of others, while Yahushua was teaching that we first need to get our hearts right and obey internally for the sake of YHWH.

The Torah has been described as: the Way, the Truth, the Light and Life (Psalms 119:142, Proverbs 6:23; Psalms 119:92). There is no coincidence that Yahushua uses these same words to refer to Himself since He was the very embodiment of the Torah. His teachings were always consistent with the written Torah and His life was a fulfillment of the Torah. As a result, those that follow Him and consider themselves to be His disciples should likewise endeavor to fulfill the Torah both in their hearts and through their lives.

7

The Disciples and the Torah

Not only was Yahushua Torah observant, but so were His disciples. The word disciple has a variety of meanings and is generally defined as follows:

1. a. One who embraces and assists in spreading the teachings of another.
   b. An active adherent, as of a movement or philosophy.
2. One of the original followers of Jesus.
3. A member of the Disciples of Christ.[52]

A disciple is a "student" or "taught one" which in Hebrew is talmidim (תלמידם). The talmidim of Yahushua did not only include the twelve but there were hundreds, if not thousands, who followed His teachings.

The Scriptures are filled with examples of how these talmidim were Torah observant. Yahushua always revered the Torah and He always observed the Torah. If there is anyone in history who understood the teachings of Yahushua as they related to the Torah, I suspect that it would be the original talmidim who followed Yahushua, observed the way He lived and heard His teachings. Those talmidim continued to observe the Torah after His death and resurrection.

The following are some clear examples from the Messianic Scriptures concerning the Sabbath observance of the original Believers.

*"Then they went home and prepared spices and perfumes. But **they rested on the Sabbath in obedience to the commandment**."* Luke 23:56.

"After the Sabbath, at dawn on the first day of the week, Mary Magdalene and the other Mary went to look at the tomb." Mattityahu 28:1. They waited to go to the tomb because they were resting, in observance of the Sabbath. Since the Sabbath ended at sundown and there were no streetlights, it would only make sense that two women would wait until sunrise to travel. These were followers of Yahushua who heard His teachings and observed His ways. If they were observing the Sabbath even after His death, when they desperately wanted to get to the tomb, then clearly they understood that the Sabbath was a continuing mandate.

An erroneous interpretation of the following passage in Acts is often used to support the belief that the Sabbath was changed to Sunday. "[7] ***Now on the first day of the week, when the disciples (talmidim) came together to break bread, Shaul, ready to depart the next day, spoke to them and continued his message until midnight.*** [8] *There were many lamps in the upper room where they were gathered together."* Acts 20:7-8. This verse is construed by some to support the change from the Sabbath (seventh day) to the so called Lord's Day (first day) since the talmidim "broke bread" on the first day of the week.

In order to properly understand this passage you need to know the correct Scriptural method of reckoning time as well as Hebraic tradition. While the modern solar calendar considers midnight to be the beginning of a

new day, the Scriptural day begins after sunset, typically when three stars are visible in the sky. Thus, the new day actually begins in the evening.

Traditionally, when the Sabbath ends at the setting of the sun on the seventh day (Saturday night) many people continue to fellowship with a meal (ie. break bread), because it is then permissible to cook. Although the setting of the sun signifies the beginning of the first day of the week and work can be done - most people would not go to work because it is dark. As a result, many would continue to fellowship and break bread after the Sabbath. The time after the Sabbath when the sun is set is called havdallah, which means "separation."

Some people observe a special ceremony to commemorate the passing of the Sabbath which is then followed by fellowship and a meal. This meal, according to tradition, is called the Melaveh Malka and it means "accompanying the queen." "Partaking in this meal is an additional way of bidding farewell to the Sabbath. According to legend, the custom originated with King David. David asked [Elohim] when he would die, and [Elohim] told him it would be on a Sabbath. From that time on, when each Sabbath was over, David made a party to celebrate his survival. The nation at large rejoiced with him and adopted the practice of celebrating the Melaveh Malka on Saturday night."[53]

This is generally what the talmidim were doing in the passage in Acts. After the Sabbath was over and it was dark, they remained together for fellowship and a meal. Shaul would be leaving the next morning at first light to continue his travels so he spent his last waking hours, which was the first day of the week, sharing and

teaching until midnight. In this particular passage a great miracle occurred when Eutychus was raised from the dead after falling out of a third story window. Understandably, nobody went to bed and they all talked until daylight. (Acts 20:9-12).

Now some might argue that these talmidim were Yisraelites and that is why they observed the Torah but Gentile converts were no different than the native Yisraelites. They were expected to go to Synagogue on the Sabbath and learn the Torah along with the Hebrew Believers. (Acts 15:19-21, see Chapter 10). The reason for this is so they could obey the Torah as all of the Assembly of Believers were expected to do. Some theologians have tried to explain this glaring contradiction in Christian history by creating an Apostolic Dispensation although that has no basis in Scripture.

The talmidim, including the Apostle Shaul, observed the Scriptural Feasts as we read in the Book of Acts. (Acts 18:21; 20:16). They did so, not to bide their time until the dispensation passed, but because that is what every Believer is expected to do. The Torah is our guide and it shows us the plan of YHWH for our lives. In fact, if the talmidim had not been obedient to the Torah and remained in Yahrushalayim for the Feast of Shavuot, also known as Pentecost, they would have missed the outpouring of the Spirit.[54]

They observed the dietary instructions, participated in the Temple Services and promoted Torah observance. In fact, Stephen (Stephanos), the first recorded martyr in the Messianic Scriptures was falsely accused of teaching against the Torah. "[12] *So they stirred up the people and the elders and the teachers of the Torah. They seized Stephanos*

and brought him before the Sanhedrin. [13] *They produced false witnesses, who testified, 'This fellow never stops speaking against this holy place and against the Torah.* [14] *For we have heard him say that this Yahushua of Nazareth will destroy this place and change the customs Mosheh handed down to us.'"* Acts 6:12-14.

It is important to note that the charges were false and the witnesses were lying. Thus Stephanos, described as being *"a man full of Elohim's grace and power"* a man who *"did great wonders and miraculous signs among the people"* (Acts 6:8) ***did not*** speak against the holy place and against the Torah. He demonstrated great wisdom and strength in spirit and evil men *"secretly persuaded some men to say, 'We have heard Stephanos speak words of blasphemy against Mosheh and against Elohim.'"* Acts 6:11.

As talmidim are we not to emulate our Messiah? Did Yahushua not tell us that we would do even greater things than Him? (Yahanan 14:12). According to Scripture He was a Torah observant Yisraelite who lived a sinless life (Ibrim (Hebrews) 4:15) without spot or blemish (1 Kepha 1:19). Should we not endeavor to follow His example?

Right about this time, you might be saying to yourself: "This sounds like legalism." It may in fact sound like legalism depending upon your definition of legalism. You see legalism is not always bad, as most Christians believe. Typically, when a Christian is confronted with the subject of obeying YHWH's commandments they will quickly retort that "This is legalism" without having the least bit of understanding what legalism means.

According to Webster's New World Dictionary, legalism is defined as either "strict adherence to the law" or "too strict adherence to the law." Applying this definition

to Torah observance we can deduce that there is a form of legalism which applies to those who diligently keep the Torah and there is another form of legalism which applies to those who go beyond what the Torah prescribes.

The Torah specifically provides: "[17] *You shall diligently keep (shamar) the commandments of YHWH your Elohim, His testimonies, and His statutes which He has commanded you.* [18] *And you shall do what is right and good in the sight of YHWH, that it may be well with you, and that you may go in and possess the good Land of which YHWH swore to your fathers,* [19] *to cast out all your enemies from before you, as YHWH has spoken.*" Devarim 6:16-19.

Here we see the word shamar again and there is nothing wrong with diligently obeying the commandments, in fact, it is required conduct. The problem is when people start adding to the Torah and taking away from the Torah by creating their own laws and then imposing those man-made commandments upon others.

This issue was a very large part of the ministry of Yahushua who was legalistic in the sense that He zealously kept the Torah of YHWH. He also spent a lot of His time pointing out the improper legalism being promulgated by the religious elite. Their form of legalism was incorrect in that they added to the Torah and were legalistic toward their own laws while neglecting the commandments of YHWH.

We see this in the religion of Judaism today. In their attempt to build a fence around the Torah,[55] the Rabbis have created their own rules and regulations which often contradict or supersede the Torah itself. They have added thousands of new requirements which can create a considerable burden for people to bear. Those who want to

be obedient often become entangled and snared in the rules of man and end up missing the blessings, freedom, rest and peace provided by the Torah. There is nothing wrong with legalism so long as it means zealously guarding and keeping the commandments of YHWH and not those of men.

The word "legalism" is not mentioned in the text of any of the Scriptures - only once when Shaul was laying out his qualifications did he use the word "legalistic." He did so when he was addressing the Philippians regarding "The Circumcision" - those who were spreading false rumors about him and his teaching as well as the false doctrine of circumcision as a prerequisite for salvation. "[2] *Watch out for those dogs, those men who do evil, those mutilators of the flesh.* [3] *For it is we who are the circumcision, we who worship by the Spirit of Elohim, who glory in Messiah Yahushua, and who put no confidence in the flesh -* [4] *though I myself have reasons for such confidence. If anyone else thinks he has reasons to put confidence in the flesh, I have more:* [5] *circumcised on the eighth day, of the people of Yisrael, of the tribe of Benjamin, a Hebrew of Hebrews; in regard to the Torah, a Pharisee;* [6] *as for zeal, persecuting the church;* ***as for legalistic righteousness, faultless.***" Philippians 3:2-6.

What Shaul is referring to in this passage is better explained by a literal translation "*according to righteousness in Torah, being blameless.*" In other words, he kept the Torah meticulously. Shaul understood that keeping the Torah did not provide the salvation that every man requires because we are all still marred by sin until there has been atonement for those sins. Therefore, he was legalistic in his adherence to the Torah, but he understood that legalistic righteousness could not save him. This may differ from

the paradigm that many people have concerning the life and teachings of Shaul. Therefore, the following chapters will take a closer look at this controversial figure and his often misunderstood teachings.

8

Shaul and the Torah

It is my hope that by this point, the reader can plainly see the value of the Torah and the need to obey the commandments. In my opinion, there is no other collection of writings which have been more misunderstood, mistranslated, misappropriated or misinterpreted than the letters of Shaul. The reason for these problems generally arise from a failure to properly appropriate the letters to their rightful place within the Scriptures and view them in their historical context.

To begin with, it is uncertain whether Shaul wrote all of the letters attributed to him.[56] Second, they were simply letters written to various assemblies of Believers often addressing very specific, and sometimes very practical issues. They were not meant to be broad theological statements which changed the Torah. In fact, if at anytime those letters in any way contradict the Torah, or the teachings of Messiah, they must be discounted or the translation must be reexamined.

I do not believe that, when properly translated, the writings of Shaul contradict the Torah or the Messiah, but sadly there are some that do. If you fall into that category

and have chosen to subscribe to the writings of a man over the commandments of Elohim, then your faith is seriously misplaced.

Since we have already established that Yahushua did not change the Torah, if you think that Shaul changed the Torah then he was a false prophet – plain and simple. If you believe that Shaul had the authority to change the Torah when the Messiah Himself did not - then you need to make a choice as the other Yahushua (Joshua) stated: "[14] *Now therefore, fear YHWH, serve Him in sincerity and in truth, and put away the gods which your fathers served on the other side of the River and in Egypt (Mitsrayim). Serve YHWH!* [15] *And if it seems evil to you to serve YHWH, choose for yourselves this day whom you will serve, whether the gods which your fathers served that were on the other side of the River, or the gods of the Amorites, in whose land you dwell. But as for me and my house, we will serve YHWH.*" Yahushua (Joshua) 24:14-15.

If you decide not to keep the Torah because of something that you read from Shaul – then you have made your choice. You have chosen to follow the interpretations of a man, not the Torah of YHWH. You have chosen to serve "*the gods which your fathers served*" and live a life of sin and lawlessness – which is the end result of disobeying the Torah. (1 Yahanan 3:4). In that event the Scriptures provide a clear description of your fate. "[26] *For if we sin willfully after we have received the knowledge of the truth, there no longer remains a sacrifice for sins,* [27] *but a certain fearful expectation of judgment, and fiery indignation which will devour the adversaries.*" Ibrim (Hebrews) 10:26-27.

Again, I do not believe that Shaul was a false prophet because I understand his teachings in their proper

context and I do not see any conflict between his writings and the Torah. Sadly, many of the false doctrines which have developed within Christianity over the centuries stem from the misinterpretation of the writings of Shaul.

During his life he had some major detractors who he referred to as "The Circumcision." This group of people taught that the physical act of circumcision was a prerequisite to salvation. Shaul taught that the circumcision of the heart was the most important circumcision and because of these teachings he was misconstrued as teaching against circumcision of the flesh and the Torah.[57]

The Scriptures are clear that although there were false rumors about Shaul, he kept the Torah and never taught otherwise. A good example was when James (Ya'akov)[58] advised Shaul to pay for four brethren as they completed their Nazirite vows. If Shaul was teaching that the Torah was abolished or unnecessary, he would not be helping others fulfill a mitzvot which is found in the Torah. (see Bemidbar 6:5-21).

Here is the text which describes that event. "[17] *And when we had come to Yahrushalayim, the brethren received us gladly.*[18] *On the following day Shaul went in with us to Ya'akov, and all the elders were present.*[19] *When he had greeted them, he told in detail those things which Elohim had done among the Gentiles through his ministry.*[20] *And when they heard it, they glorified the Master. And they said to him, 'You see, brother, how many myriads of Yahudim there are who have believed, and they are all zealous for the Torah;* [21] *but they have been informed about you that you teach all the Yahudim who are among the Gentiles to forsake Mosheh (Torah), saying that they ought not to circumcise their children nor to walk according to the customs.*[22] *What then? The assembly must certainly meet,*

for they will hear that you have come.[23] *Therefore do what we tell you: We have four men who have taken a vow.*[24] *Take them and be purified with them, and pay their expenses so that they may shave their heads, and that all may know that those things of which they were informed concerning you are nothing, but that you yourself also walk orderly and keep the Torah.*'" Acts 21:17-24.

"[26] *Then Shaul took the men, and the next day, having been purified with them, entered the Temple to announce the expiration of the days of purification, at which time an offering should be made for each one of them.* [27] *When the seven days were nearly over, some Yahudim from the province of Asia saw Shaul at the Temple. They stirred up the whole crowd and seized him,* [28] *shouting, 'Men of Yisrael, help us! This is the man who teaches all men everywhere against our people and our Torah and this place. And besides, he has brought Greeks into the Temple area and defiled this holy place.'* [29] *(They had previously seen Trophimus the Ephesian in the city with Shaul and assumed that Shaul had brought him into the Temple area.)*" Acts 21:26-29.

Interestingly, the completion of the Nazirite vow involved sacrifices, a concept which completely flies in the face of common Christian doctrine that the sacrificial system was abolished. Shaul's conduct was specifically intended to make a public affirmation that he supported the Temple system, and the entire Torah for that matter.

Shaul observed the Torah and assisted others in observing the Torah. The accusations being made against him were false and he goes on to defend himself in the rest of the account. The reason why he was in the Temple was to make a statement that he was not teaching against the Torah. This would appear to put to rest the entire argument that Shaul taught that the Gentiles did not have

to obey the Torah, but sadly people continue to interpret his letters as teaching otherwise.

Another interesting part of this passage is the fact that Shaul is submitted to the authority of Ya'akov and the Elders of the Assembly in Yahrushalayim.[59] He was not a maverick changing the faith or starting a new religion. He was called to the Gentiles but he reported to Yahrushalayim and was in one accord with the brethren in Yahrushalayim. Shaul obeyed the Torah and always encouraged others to obey the Torah. He described the Torah in the letter to the Romans as Holy, Just, Good and Spiritual.

He also stated that: "[16] *All Scripture is given by inspiration of Elohim, and is profitable for doctrine, for reproof, for correction, for instruction in righteousness,* [17] *that the man of Elohim may be complete, thoroughly equipped for every good work.*" 2 Timothy 3:16-17. Of course the only Scriptures that he could have been talking about were the Torah, the Prophets and the Writings (Tanak) - there were no "New Testament" Scriptures in existence.

Concerning himself and the Torah he stated the following: "*But this I confess to you, that according to the Way which they call a sect, so I worship the Elohim of my fathers,* ***believing all things which are written in the Torah and in the Prophets.***" Acts 24:14. "*Neither against the Torah of the Yahudim, nor against the Temple, nor against Caesar have I offended in anything at all.*" Acts 25:8. "*For I delight in the Torah of Elohim . . .*" Romans 7:22.

At this point it is worth reiterating that Shaul wrote about his Torah observant heritage describing himself as "*a Hebrew of Hebrews, according to Torah a Pharisee . . . concerning the righteousness which is in the Torah, blameless*"

Philippians 3:5-6. In other words, he was a highly trained ultra-conservative Torah observant Hebrew of the Pharisaic Sect and he was not ashamed to disclose that information. Nothing in his life, ministry, statements or teachings ever changed that fact. He loved his Messiah and he lived and taught the Torah of his Messiah.

9

The Teachings of Shaul

As previously stated, many of Shaul's teachings are used to support a variety of doctrines which contradict the Torah and even the teachings of Yahushua. It is for this reason that some look to Shaul as the founder of a new religion called Christianity.

The Messiah did not come to start a new religion, rather He came to straighten out His people and mediate the Renewed Covenant. Likewise, Shaul had no intention of establishing a new religion. He spent his time attempting to explain the work of the Messiah, often to a people who had no real experience or training in the Torah. Shaul was a brilliant Torah scholar and it is necessary to have an understanding of the Torah in order to fully understand his teachings

This is why Kepha specifically warned people concerning Shaul's writings: "[15] *and consider that the longsuffering of our Master is salvation — as also our beloved brother Shaul, according to the wisdom given to him, has written to you,* [16] *as also in all his epistles, speaking in them of these things, in which are some things hard to understand, which untaught and unstable people twist to their own destruction, as*

they do also the rest of the Scriptures." 2 Kepha 3:15-16.

This is exactly what has happened over the centuries. People have twisted the epistles as well as the rest of the Scriptures to meet their own end – they do so to their own destruction. Much of the time this is done because they do not understand the significance of the Torah nor do they understand the context of Shaul's writings. Sadly, they also teach their lies to the unwary and untaught who often accept them out of ignorance.

Without a fundamental understanding of the Torah and the work of the Messiah this is easy enough to do. Regrettably it is not possible to fully examine all of the writings of Shaul in this book – the subject is simply too vast. What we can do is take a look at some specific examples of his teachings and see how they have been twisted – as described by Kepha.

Prior to his eyes being opened to the Messiahship of Yahushua, Shaul was potentially destined to become the head of the Sanhedrin - the High Court of Yisrael. On the Road to Damascus, the Scriptures provide a powerful meeting between Yahushua and Shaul.[60] He was not converted to Christianity during this

encounter as many teach - rather he was confronted by the Messiah and, while "blinded by the light" his eyes were opened concerning the fact that Yahushua was the Messiah. It is then believed by some that he went to Mount Sinai in Arabia where his doctrine was corrected. The same place where Mosheh and Elijah (Eliyahu)[61] met with YHWH is likely the place where Shaul met with YHWH.[62]

After this experience he understood that the Torah was intended to lead men to the Messiah - Who had come to restore the Kingdom which included regathering the lost sheep of the house of Yisrael that had been scattered amongst the Gentiles.[63] Thus a man who arguably knew the Torah better than anybody was on a mission to reveal the Messiah to the Gentiles, people who had little to no knowledge of the Torah.

Interestingly, the primary tool that Shaul used to prove that Yahushua was the Messiah was the Torah and the Prophets. "*So when they had appointed him a day, many came to him at his lodging, to whom he explained and solemnly testified of the kingdom of Elohim, persuading them concerning Yahushua from both the Torah of Mosheh and the Prophets, from morning till evening.*" Acts 28:23. In fact, most of his writings could easily be classified as Torah commentary. They certainly were not considered to be Scripture when he wrote them and there were no Gospels to refer people to. The only Scriptures that existed were found in the Tanak.

Many of Shaul's letters to various assemblies of Believers throughout the Mediterranean region have since been "canonized"[64] and therefore treated as Scriptures. These writings are often used to support the argument that the Torah has been done away with or does not apply to Christians and Shaul is credited with many sayings which people parrot in an effort to justify their rejection of the Torah. One of the major retorts that a Christian will provide when confronted with the issue of the Torah will undoubtedly be that the Torah was "nailed to the cross."

This concept derives from Colossians 2:14 which reads as follows: "[14] *having wiped out the handwriting of*

requirements that was against us, which was contrary to us. And He has taken it out of the way, having nailed it to the cross (stake)."[65] In this particular letter Shaul gave a wonderfully concise description of how we are saved and shows the spiritual meaning and significance of the Torah. For the purposes of this discussion we need to focus on the phrase "*the handwriting of requirements that was against us.*"

The Amplified Bible elaborates a bit more on this text. "*Having cancelled and blotted out and wiped away the handwriting of the note (bond) with its legal decrees and demands which was in force and stood against us (hostile to us). This [note with its regulations, decrees, and demands] He set aside and cleared completely out of our way by nailing it to [His] cross.*" Colossians 2:14 AMP.

Another version gives us an even more vivid look at the meaning of this passage. "*Having blotted out the certificate of debt against us (the record of all the sins we did) - by the dogmas – which stood against us. And he has taken it out of the way having nailed it to the stake.*" Colossians 2:14 The Scriptures.

When we look at the Greek we see that Shaul was talking about forgiving our sins by nailing them to the stake. We all have sinned and that sin requires payment - our sin becomes a legal debt or bond, which must be paid. Yahushua paid that debt on the stake and He nailed our list of sins to the stake, thus blotting them out.

This is a good example of why it is important to understand the Scriptures in context. In the days of Yahushua, when a criminal was executed on a stake, it was common practice to nail a list of his crimes on the stake, as was done with Yahushua. (see Mattithyahu 27:37).

The notion that Shaul was referring to the Torah

has no basis in Scripture. On the other hand, the translation that our sins were blotted out and nailed to the stake is completely consistent with Scriptures and the culture of the days of Yahushua.

This is the same concept that David (Dawid)[66] was referring to when he prayed: "*Hide your face from my sins and blot out all my iniquity.*" Tehillim 51:9 NIV. It is also exactly what the Prophet Yirmeyahu (Jeremiah)[67] was referring to when He prayed to the Almighty regarding his accusers. "*But you know, O YHWH, all their plots to kill me. Do not forgive their crimes or blot out their sins from your sight.*" Yirmeyahu 18:23. They both refer to sins (crimes) and blotting out that iniquity (sin). We need our sins blotted out that we might live. Thus it was not the Torah that was nailed to the stake but rather the list of our transgressions against the Torah which would require us to be punished.

If you can get past the "nailed to the cross" issue with a Christian who does not follow Torah you will probably be met with the argument that we are no longer "under the law." This notion comes from a number of different quotes from Shaul's writings. In Romans 6:14-15 we read: "[14] *For sin shall not have dominion over you, for you are not under law but under grace.* [15] *What then? Shall we sin because we are not under law but under grace? Certainly not!*" *NKJV.*

Some interpret this passage to mean that we are not subject to the Torah, but only grace. If this were true it would completely fly in the face of the entire Tanak as well as the teachings of the Messiah and His talmidim. What Shaul is saying here is really quite simple. Since the definition of sin is a violation of the Torah, being under

the Torah cannot possibly be the same as being obedient to the Torah.

If you are a Believer who has been saved by grace then you are covered by the atoning blood of Messiah and your sins have been blotted out. If so, then you are not subject to the punishment for violating the Torah. Therefore, when Shaul refers to being "under the Torah" he is talking about being in a state where you are subject to the Torah's punishments.

If you have been redeemed then you are not under the Torah in the sense of being subject to the punishment of death for violating the Torah, but under grace which is a state of being redeemed by the free gift given by Messiah. As if to ensure that there is no question on this point Shaul continued by stating in verse 15: "*Shall we sin because we are not under law (Torah) but under grace? Certainly not!*" He also stated in Romans 3:31: "*Do we then make void the Torah through faith? Certainly not! On the contrary, we establish the Torah.*"

There are many other quotes from Shaul which are taken out of context and misappropriated to support the notion that the Torah has somehow been abolished or is not applicable to certain groups of Believers. There is no question that when you read the writings of Shaul in their proper context you will find that He supports the Torah.

10

The Jerusalem Council

When a person receives forgiveness from YHWH it is essential that they learn and observe the Torah - as obedient children - so that they do not continue in lawlessness and thereby "*trample the blood of the Messiah*" as was warned in Hebrews (Ibrim).[68] This was clear to the early Believers because they were Torah observant Yisraelites who were "*zealous for the Torah.*" (Acts 21:20). It was never an issue whether to observe the Torah, they just did it because they knew it was the right thing to do and it never conflicted with their belief in Messiah.

Torah observance only became an issue when Gentiles began believing in the Messiah. They were saved by faith and received the promise of the Spirit although some were being incorrectly instructed that they had to also be circumcised in order to be saved. Much of the controversy addressed by Shaul in his letters to the Romans and the Galatians revolved around this issue and it was one of the underlying reasons why he wrote his letters to the various assemblies.[69]

The matter was also dealt with by the leaders of the assembly in Yahrushalayim, which resulted in what

is commonly referred to as "The Letter to the Gentile Converts." It is believed that the Council met at about 49 C.E. and the issue is detailed in Acts 15. I have inserted most of the text so the reader can get a complete picture of the problem that was being addressed and the solution that was reached.

"[1] *Some men came down from Judea to Antioch and were teaching the brothers:* ***'Unless you are circumcised, according to the custom taught by Mosheh, you cannot be saved.'*** [2] *This brought Shaul and Barnabas into sharp dispute and debate with them. So Shaul and Barnabas were appointed, along with some other believers, to go up to Yahrushalayim to see the apostles and elders about this question.* [3] *The assembly sent them on their way, and as they traveled through Phoenicia and Samaria, they told how the Gentiles had been converted. This news made all the brothers very glad.* [4] *When they came to Yahrushalayim, they were welcomed by the assembly and the apostles and elders, to whom they reported everything Elohim had done through them.* [5] *Then some of the believers who belonged to the party of the Pharisees stood up and said, 'The Gentiles must be circumcised and required to obey the Torah of Mosheh.'*" Acts 15:1-5.

The dynamics of this conflict are very interesting. There were representatives of Believers present from different sects, including the Pharisees - possibly some of the same Pharisees that heard the teachings and the rebukes of Yahushua. The issue here is Gentile conversion, not into the religion of Judaism or Christianity, but into the Commonwealth of Yisrael. The Gentile converts were leaving a life of paganism and lawlessness and entering into the Kingdom of YHWH.[70] The debate involved circumcision as a requirement for salvation (Acts 15:1 and Acts 15:5), not whether Gentile converts should observe

the Torah. Some from the Pharisee Sect were instructing new converts that they needed to be circumcised ***in order to receive salvation***. For those who think that this was a ridiculous notion - think again.

The Torah frequently mentioned the Gentiles and Gentile converts by referring to the alien, foreigner, stranger and sojourner. YHWH always made room for the Gentile to be included within Yisrael. The notion that the Torah was only for the "Jew" is simply untrue, because there were always Gentile converts sojourning within the Nation of Yisrael. From the day they left Egypt (Mitsrayim)[71] with the "mixed multitude" to the day they crossed the Jordan (Yarden) River. The Torah was always applicable to non-native Yisraelites who believed in YHWH Elohim. "[33] *And if a stranger dwells with you in your land, you shall not mistreat him.*[34] *The stranger who dwells among you shall be to you as one born among you, and you shall love him as yourself; for you were strangers in the land of Mitsrayim: I am YHWH your Elohim.*" Vayiqra 19:33-34.

The Torah applied to the stranger just as it did to the native Yisraelite so long as the person desired to dwell with the set apart people and live a life of obedience to YHWH. "*An alien living among you who wants to celebrate YHWH's Passover must do so in accordance with its rules and regulations. You must have the same regulations for the alien and the native-born.*" Bemidbar 9:14. The strangers were also subject to punishment for disobeying the Torah, even unto death. (Vayiqra 20:2).

The common belief that the Torah only applied to native Yisraelites is absolutely false. Anybody who wanted to dwell with Yisrael and sojourn with YHWH was required to obey the rules of the kingdom, which

were found in the Torah. They were subject to the same benefits and punishments - the same blessings and curses that applied to the Children of Yisrael because they had become part of Yisrael.

The Pharisees and other Believers who Shaul referred to as "The Circumcision" taught that Gentiles needed to be circumcised in order to be saved, largely because of the commandment in the Torah concerning Passover (Pesach)[72] which reads as follows: "[43] *And YHWH said to Mosheh and Aaron (Aharon), '**This is the ordinance of the Passover: no foreigner shall eat it.*** [44] *But every man's servant who is bought for money, when you have circumcised him, then he may eat it.*[45] *A sojourner and a hired servant shall not eat it.*[46] *In one house it shall be eaten; you shall not carry any of the flesh outside the house, nor shall you break one of its bones.*[47] *All the congregation of Yisrael shall keep it.*[48] *And when a stranger dwells with you and wants to keep the Pesach to YHWH, let all his males be circumcised, and then let him come near and keep it; and he shall be as a native of the Land.* ***For no uncircumcised person shall eat it.***[49] ***one Torah shall be for the native-born and for the stranger who dwells among you.***" Shemoth 12:43-49.

Therefore, those whom Shaul called "The Circumcision" believed that if circumcision was required in the Torah to partake in the Pesach and be considered a native of the land (ie. native Yisraelite), then the same must hold true for followers of the Messiah. They believed that Gentile converts had to become part of "Native Yisrael" before they could partake of the Messiah. This teaching resulted from a failure to understand that the redemption provided by the Messiah was the same as the redemption provided by YHWH through Mosheh – only this time it was our souls being redeemed and not our bodies.

The redemption offered by Yahushua, and the Renewed Covenant - which He mediated - involved circumcising our hearts. With that in mind, let us continue with the Yahrushalayim Council.

"[6] *The apostles and elders met to consider this question.*
[7] *After much discussion, Kepha got up and addressed them: 'Brothers, you know that some time ago Elohim made a choice among you that the Gentiles might hear from my lips the message of the good news and believe.* [8] *Elohim, who knows the heart, showed that He accepted them by giving the Holy Spirit to them, just as He did to us.* [9] *<u>He made no distinction between us and them, for He purified their hearts by faith</u>.* [10] *Now then, why do you try to test Elohim by putting on the necks of the disciples a yoke that neither we nor our fathers have been able to bear?* [11] *No!* ***We believe it is through the grace of our Master Yahushua that we are saved, just as they are.***" Acts 15:6-11.

Again, the issue was whether the Gentiles needed to be circumcised in their flesh to be saved, not whether they were to obey the Torah. Obedience to the Torah was presumed. It is an undisputed fact that all of the leaders at the Yahrushalayim Council were Torah observant. What then is this yoke that Kepha is referring to? It is not the Torah, but rather the myriad of rules, regulations and traditions which the religious leaders had been heaping upon native Yisraelites and converts for centuries - that same yoke which the Messiah was referring to when he spoke to those who were burdened and heavy laden.

A good example of the yoke of bondage created by men can be seen in the Sabbath. The Torah includes very few commands relating to the Sabbath while religious men like the Pharisees added hundreds - if not thousands - of man-made regulations. This obviously did not result

in the rest intended by YHWH. What YHWH intended for our benefit, man turned into bondage because it was hard enough to know all of the added regulations, let alone obey them.

YHWH set Yisrael free from bondage as well as the mixed multitude that left Mitsrayim with them. "[13] *I am YHWH your Elohim, who brought you out of Mitrayim so that you would no longer be slaves to the Mitsrites; <u>I broke the bars of your yoke and enabled you to walk with heads held high</u>.*" Vayiqra 26:1-22. Notice that YHWH does not consider His commandments to be a yoke of slavery. He brought Yisrael out of Mitsrayim, broke the yoke of slavery and expected them to obey the Torah which does not involve putting them back into bondage.

The Torah is for free men and women - it is not meant to make them into slaves. In fact, most Scriptures which refer to a yoke refer to slavery or oppression brought on by man. YHWH is gentle with us and lifts the yoke from our necks. "[1] *When Yisrael was a child, I loved him, and out of Mitsrayim I called my son.* [2] *But the more I called Yisrael, the further they went from me. They sacrificed to the Baals and they burned incense to images.* [3] *It was I who taught Ephraim to walk, taking them by the arms; but they did not realize it was I who healed them.* [4] ***I led them with cords of human kindness, with ties of love; I lifted the yoke from their neck and bent down to feed them.***" Hosea (Hoshea) 11:1-4.

Never does YHWH refer to His instructions as a heavy yoke, certainly not a burden. In fact, He describes His instruction as "*cords of human kindness*" and "*ties of love.*" In other words, they are meant to guide us in the way we should walk. In that same vein Yahushua, reading from the Book of Isaiah (Yeshayahu)[73] proclaimed: "[18] *The*

Spirit of YHWH is upon Me, because He has anointed Me to preach the good news to the poor; He has sent Me to heal the brokenhearted, ***to proclaim liberty to the captives*** *and recovery of sight to the blind,* ***to set at liberty those who are oppressed;*** [19] *To proclaim the acceptable year of YHWH.*" Luke 4:18-19.

This is further affirmed by Shaul in his Epistle to the Galatians. "***It is for freedom that Messiah has set us free. Stand firm, then, and do not let yourselves be burdened again by a yoke of slavery.***" Galatians 5:1. The yoke of slavery that Shaul is referring to is not the Torah. The context of this Scripture is crystal clear - he is talking about the teaching of circumcision as a prerequisite for salvation which then leads to a doctrine of justification by works.[74]

It is important to realize that the Torah was never believed to be a burden and it was Yahushua that spoke of giving "*a yoke which is easy and a burden which is light.*" This was declared in the Messianic Scriptures when Yahushua said: "[28] *Come to me, all you who are weary and burdened, and I will give you rest.* [29] *Take my yoke upon you and learn from me, for I am gentle and humble in heart, and you will find rest for your souls.* [30] ***For my yoke is easy and my burden is light.***" Mattithyahu 11:28-30 NIV.

He also said that: "[31] *If you abide in* ***My Word,*** *you are My disciples indeed.* [32] *And you shall know the truth, and* ***the truth shall make you free.***" Yahanan 8:31-32 NKJV. The Torah is His Word and ***the Torah is truth.*** (Tehillim 119:142; Yahanan 17:17). Therefore the Torah shall make you free. Ya'akov describes the Torah as "*the perfect Torah of liberty.*" Ya'akov 1:25.

Mosheh said that keeping the Torah was not too difficult. "***Now what I am commanding you today is not too difficult for you or beyond your reach.***" Devarim 30:11. "*For I*

command you today to love YHWH your Elohom, to walk in his ways, and to keep His commands, decrees and laws; ***then you will live and increase****, and YHWH your Elohim will bless you in the land you are entering to possess.*" Devarim 30:16. Yahanan affirms that the Torah is not a burden when he stated: "*For this is the love of Elohim, that we keep His commandments. And* ***His commandments are not burdensome.***" 1 Yahanan 5:3.

Yahushua continued the purpose and plan of YHWH, but instead of freeing Yisrael from physical bondage, as they were anticipating, He freed them from spiritual bondage. At no time was Torah observance considered to be bondage - it is always men that put other men into bondage - not YHWH. Our Elohim desires for us to willingly become His Bondservants, He never indentures someone against their will. Therefore it is not proper to speak of His Torah as a burden or a yoke which would enslave a person – to do so would be clear error. In fact, the Scriptures attest to the contrary. "[44] *So shall I keep thy Torah continually for ever and ever.* [45] *And I will walk at liberty: for I seek thy precepts.*" Tehillim 119:44-45.

You have to be free to obey the Torah and if you cannot obey the Torah then you must not be free. There is an important distinction between physical bondage and spiritual bondage. Many Christians cannot understand this concept, just as some early talmidim did not understand. "[33] *They answered him, 'We are Avraham's descendants and have never been slaves of anyone. How can you say that we shall be set free?'* [34] *Yahushua replied, 'I tell you the truth, everyone who sins is a slave to sin.* [35] *Now a slave has no permanent place in the family, but a son belongs to it forever.* [36] *So if the Son sets you free, you will be free indeed.'*" Yahanan 8:33-36.

The question then is: Are you free to obey? If you are not obeying the Torah, you are living in a state of lawlessness - which is sin. If you are living in sin, then you are not free, but rather you are a slave to sin!

I live in the United States of America which is, by most accounts, the beacon of freedom throughout the world. America is probably considered the freest society ever to exist in the history of the world. At the same time, we have more laws than any other nation in the history of the world. Therefore, is it fair to assume that the existence of laws puts us in bondage? Absolutely not! It is the system that puts people into bondage, not the law. America is a Republic, with a constitution that provides rights and privileges to its' citizens and establishes a framework for an organized and free society. Laws are meant to delineate between conduct which is acceptable and conduct which is prohibited - this is supposed to be for the protection of those who dwell in American society.[75]

Compare this to military dictatorships, socialist, communist, fascist and radical Islamic states which provide little to no rights for their citizens. There are laws in every nation and while some nations are considered free others are considered oppressive. In the case of America it is the law, in particular, the Constitution which provides us with our freedom.

Regrettably, over the centuries, men and special interest groups have heaped on additional laws which have stripped away many of our freedoms and altered the

original intent of the Constitution just as men, including the Pharisees added to and, in effect, altered the Torah which was meant for a freed people. It is the failure to understand the Torah and its purpose which has led to such confusion in Christianity.

The Torah was provided by YHWH to Yisrael and subsequently all of mankind to lead them in the path of righteousness. It is meant to teach all mankind how YHWH desires for us to live. It sets boundaries for those who follow YHWH which are meant for their protection and well being – it leads to life.

Now let us continue with the solution to the problem that was resolved by the Yahrushalayim Council. "[12] *The whole assembly became silent as they listened to Barnabas and Shaul telling about the miraculous signs and wonders Elohim had done among the Gentiles through them.* [13] *When they finished, Ya'akov spoke up: Brothers, listen to me.* [14] *Simon has described to us how Elohim at first showed his concern by taking from the Gentiles a people for himself.* [15] *The words of the prophets are in agreement with this, as it is written:* [16] *'After this I will return and rebuild Dawid's fallen tabernacle. Its ruins I will rebuild, and I will restore it,* [17] *that the remnant of men may seek YHWH, and all the Gentiles who bear My Name, says YHWH, who does these things'* [18] *that have been known for ages.* [19] *It is my judgment, therefore, that we should not make it difficult for the Gentiles who are turning to Elohim.* [20] *Instead we should write to them, telling them to abstain from food polluted by idols, from sexual immorality, from the meat of strangled animals and from blood.* [21] ***For Mosheh (Torah) has been preached in every city from the earliest times and is read in the synagogues on every Sabbath.*** [22] *Then the apostles and elders, with the whole assembly, decided to choose some of their own*

men and send them to Antioch with Shaul and Barnabas. They chose Judas (called Barsabba) and Silas, two men who were leaders among the brothers. [23] *With them they sent the following letter: The apostles and elders, your brothers, To the Gentile believers in Antioch, Syria and Cilicia: Greetings.* [24] *We have heard that some went out from us without our authorization and disturbed you, troubling your minds by what they said.* [25] *So we all agreed to choose some men and send them to you with our dear friends Barnabas and Shaul -* [26] *men who have risked their lives for the Name of our Master Yahushua Messiah.* [27] *Therefore we are sending Judas and Silas to confirm by word of mouth what we are writing.* [28] *It seemed good to the Set Apart Spirit and to us not to burden you with anything beyond the following necessities:* [29] *You are to abstain from food sacrificed to idols, from blood, from the meat of strangled animals and from sexual immorality. You will do well to avoid these things. Farewell."* Acts 15:12-29.

Therefore, the problem presented at the Yahrushalayim Council was that there were some who were troubling the Gentile converts by instructing them that they needed to be circumcised in order to be converted and receive salvation. In essence, they were making circumcision a prerequisite to salvation. This was an error and the solution was to give the Gentile converts what appear to be four *necessities* which were immediate mandates to obey as Gentiles came to the truth.

This is perfectly understandable since most Gentile converts would have been unfamiliar with the Torah and to immediately inundate them with the entire Torah might have proven to be overwhelming for some. Gentiles were generally considered "unclean" by Yisraelites who were living set apart lives to a Holy

Elohim. It was important for the Gentile converts to stop living like pagans so that they could assemble together with their Torah observant Yisraelite brethren. The elders in Yahrushalayim intended this to be a starting point for new converts, but the Christian "Church"[76] has grabbed hold of this passage in an attempt to prove that *only* four commandments apply to Gentile Converts.

It is interesting how some who try to justify lawlessness (not obeying the Torah) use this as their basis when it actually does the exact opposite. They say that Yahushua nailed the Torah to the cross and it is no more, but if Yahushua had actually nailed the Torah to the cross and done away with the Torah then the Elders would not have given these four commandments for the Gentiles to obey because that would have been "putting them under the Law" when they were supposed to be "under grace."

So there is no confusion, these four requirements given in the Letter to the Gentile converts are all commandments found within the Torah. They were not new commandments created by the Elders. What Ya'akov did was use wisdom - he knew that the Hebrew Believers had been steeped in Torah their entire lives. The Gentiles, on the other hand, came out of pagan cultures which were completely foreign to righteous, Torah observant lifestyles.

They certainly were not able to assimilate overnight so Ya'akov gave them some important basics to begin with. This was done with the understanding that: "*Mosheh has been preached in every city from the earliest times and is read in the synagogues (assemblies) on every Sabbath.*" Acts 15:21. In other words, get them into the community of Believers, give them some essential basics and direct them

into the assembly every Sabbath - not Sunday - where the Torah is read and taught so they can learn and grow.

The reason that the specific edict was issued was because it was dealing with the pagan temple progression and was warning against those things which would happen in the typical pagan temple ritual. A person involved in pagan temple worship would usually go to the temple and fornicate, then a sacrifice would be made to the pagan god or goddess which would often be eaten along with its' blood. This entire process was an abomination and in direct contradiction to the worship prescribed by YHWH. As a result, the first thing that Gentile converts needed to

do was avoid the pagan worship system. Conversion always results in a change of lifestyle and the Letter to the Gentile converts was intended to get them out of the pagan system that they were so accustomed and "clean them up" so that they could join with the set apart Assembly.

Customarily, every Yisraelite assembly, in every city, in every nation follows the Torah cycle each year. The Torah is divided into portions so that in the course of a year they go through the entire Torah. When the cycle is completed, the Torah scroll is rolled back on Simchot Torah and the cycle begins anew. Since there were not any bound "Bibles"[77] in existence, and very few Torah Scrolls for that matter, the assembly (synagogue)[78] was the place one would go outside of Yahrushalayim to hear, read and study the Torah. The intention was that the Gentile converts would hear, read and study the Torah to build their knowledge and increase their obedience - it was not meant to limit the Gentiles to only four commandments.

I have heard it preached from Christian pulpits that Christians need only obey the four necessities outlined in Acts 15. This shows a serious lack of understanding of the context of this Scripture portion and the history of what was occurring within the early Assembly of Believers. It also does not make any sense whatsoever. Do they actually believe that YHWH has established two classes of Believers: 1) The First Class Believers with Hebrew blood that obey all the commandments and get all the blessings, and 2) The Second Class Gentile Believers who only have to obey 4 commandments and who will obviously either a.) miss out on much of the blessings which YHWH has for His people, or b.) get all the blessings by only obeying a fraction of the Torah.[79]

This type of thinking is seriously flawed. Does it mean that Christians can murder, steal, covet, take YHWH's Name in vain etc.? Of course not, the Ten Commandments (Ten Words) were straightforward enough that those were probably the first things that a Gentile convert was taught. I do not believe any Christian would argue that they do not have to obey the Ten Commandments. Therefore, there are at least fourteen commandments that a Gentile convert must obey which already shoots down the theories that "we're not under the Torah so we do not have to obey the Torah" or "the Torah was nailed to the cross and was abolished" or "Gentiles only have to obey four commandments" or "Yahushua fulfilled the Torah, so we don't have to obey the Torah anymore."

If we look further at the four necessities outlined in Acts 15 we will see that they include much more than just four prohibited acts. They generally encompass what is

commonly referred to as "The Heart of the Torah" which is located in Vayiqra 17 through Vayiqra 20.

The first of the four prohibitions was food sacrificed to idols or more specifically - the defilements of idols. To many people this seems like a very strange prohibition because we live in a day when paganism is much more veiled than it used to be. According to the Didache, an early writing attributed to Belivers, it was described as "worship of dead gods."[80]

There is a good discussion of this topic in 1 Corinthians 8 – 10 when Shaul addressed the subject with the Corinthians. It may be helpful to look at some commentary on this passage which details some of the pagan practices in the Corinthian culture.

> " . . . it must be observed that it was a custom among the heathens to make feasts on their sacrifices, and not only to eat themselves, but invite their friends to partake with them. These were usually kept in the temple, where the sacrifice was offered (v. 10), and, if any thing was left when the feast ended, it was usual to carry away a portion to their friends . . . feasts . . . were always accounted, among the heathen, sacred and religious things, so that they were wont to sacrifice before all their feasts; and it was accounted a very profane thing among them . . . to eat at their private tables any meat whereof they had not first sacrificed on such occasions . . . In this circumstance of things, while Christians lived among idolaters, had many relations and friends that were such,

> with whom they must keep up acquaintance and maintain good neighbourhood, and therefore have occasion to eat at their tables, what should they do if any thing that had been sacrificed should be set before them? What, if they should be invited to feast with them in their temples? It seems as if some of the Corinthians had imbibed an opinion that even this might be done, because they knew an idol was nothing in the world, v. 4. The apostle seems to answer more directly to the case (ch. 10), and here to argue, upon supposition of their being right in this thought, against their abuse of their liberty to the prejudice of others; but he plainly condemns such liberty in ch. 10. The apostle introduces his discourse with some remarks about knowledge that seem to carry in them a censure of such pretences to knowledge as I have mentioned: We know, says the apostle, that we all have knowledge (v. 1); as if he had said, 'You who take such liberty are not the only knowing persons; we who abstain know as much as you of the vanity of idols, and that they are nothing; but we know too that the liberty you take is very culpable, and that even lawful liberty must be used with charity and not to the prejudice of weaker brethren.'[81]

Thus we see that some Corinthian Believers continued to participate in idolatry claiming that it was alright because they "knew" that the idols were not real

gods. The problem is that this particular prohibition is not strictly limited to meat, but rather idolatry as a whole, which is considered to be spiritual whoredom. This was specifically prohibited in Shemot 34:15-16. YHWH established a sacrificial system and provided for eating meat from His sacrifices which was considered to be an integral part of the worship.

If we look at Pesach, we see that there was a lamb for every house. The Yisraelites would bring a lamb without blemish to the Tabernacle, the Mishkan or the Temple (depending on the time period) and they would offer it as a sacrifice in obedience and worship to YHWH. After the first Pesach, they would not sacrifice in their homes or any other place except the place where YHWH would choose as a dwelling for His Name. (Devarim 16:2-6). They would then take the meat of their sacrifice and eat it with their families and even friends. This was a sacred and holy act of obedience and worship which was performed at a time prescribed by YHWH.

The pagans had their own system of sacrificial offerings which was nothing short of an abomination. While the idols themselves were nothing - the process was a perversion of the system that YHWH had established and it was simply inappropriate for the Children of YHWH to be partaking in idolatry.

This is similar to what Aharon did when he built

the golden calf and then declared a feast to YHWH. "[4] *And he received the gold from their hand, and he fashioned it with an engraving tool, and made a molded calf. Then they said, '<u>This is your god, O</u>*

Yisrael, that brought you out of the land of Mitsrayim!' [5] *So when Aharon saw it, he built an altar before it. And Aharon made a proclamation and said, 'Tomorrow is a feast to YHWH.'* [6] *Then they rose early on the next day, offered burnt offerings, and brought peace offerings; and the people sat down to eat and drink, and rose up to play.*" Shemot 32:4-6. Aharon mixed pagan gods with the worship of YHWH which is exactly what is referred to by the prohibition against meat sacrificed to idols.

In Vayiqra 17 YHWH commands that the Children of Yisrael and the foreigner who dwells among them (this would correspond with a Gentile who has turned to YHWH) no longer slaughter a bull or a lamb or a goat outside the camp. All sacrifices must be brought to the door of the Tent of Meeting as an offering to YHWH before the Dwelling Place of YHWH. The blood of the sacrifice is to be sprinkled on the altar of YHWH at the door of the Tent of Meeting and the fat was to be burned for a sweet fragrance to YHWH. This is the way that YHWH directed gifts, sacrifices and worship.

Any man, be he Yisraelite or a foreigner, who chose not to offer gifts, sacrifices or worship in accordance to YHWH's directives was considered an idolater. In other words, if he chose to do it his way instead of YHWH's way - then he was to be cut off - it was not considered proper worship of YHWH but rather whoring with demons.

The application to the present is compelling and powerful. We need to search our hearts and examine our conduct to determine if we are worshipping YHWH in accordance with His directives, ordinances and commandments or whether we are worshipping Him in

our own way or in some fashion which was taught to us or which we inherited. We must make certain that our gifts, sacrifices and worship line up with His commandments and we must not be participating in pagan practices which may seem harmless on the surface, but which are actually offensive to YHWH.[82]

We read in the Scriptures that the Corinthian Assembly believed that they were mature and they relied upon their "knowledge" that the idols were not real. As a result of this knowledge, they believed that their partaking of the food sacrificed to the idols was harmless. Shaul taught otherwise and we would do well to heed his teaching on this matter because it applies just as much to modern day Believers as it did to those in the past.

The knowledge of the Corinthian Believers is the same knowledge that many Christians share concerning

the fact that Easter derives from an ancient fertility rite and Christmas is the birthday celebration of pagan sun gods. They color eggs and set up Nimrod trees in accordance with the pagan traditions. Many participate out of ignorance but others know full well the origins of these practices but consider it to be harmless. Sadly - <u>they are idolaters and their behavior is an abomination to YHWH</u>.

These words apply just as much to modern Christianity as they did to the Corinthians. "[16] *And what agreement has the Temple of Elohim with idols? For you are the Temple of the living Elohim. As Elohim has said: I will dwell in them and walk among them. I will be their Elohim, and they*

shall be My people. [17] *Therefore* ***come out from among them and be separate, says YHWH. Do not touch what is unclean, and I will receive you.*** [18] *I will be a Father to you, and you shall be My sons and daughters, says YHWH Almighty."* 2 Corinthians 6:16-18.

The Torah includes at least 53 general commandments related to idolatry alone - not to mention those related to sacrifices which are acceptable to YHWH. Therefore, there are at least 53 commandments in the Torah which are covered by the first directive which was given in the Letter to the Gentile converts by the Yahrushalayim Council.

The second and third prohibitions which were listed in the Letter to the Gentile converts can be viewed as one category. Strangled animals and blood both deal with kosher dietary instructions which are found in the Torah, although blood is treated separate from food since the Scriptures tells us that "*the life is in the blood.*" (Devarim 12:23).

It is interesting to note that fifty percent of the essential directives given to the Gentile converts deals with kosher dietary matters. Kosher, or better yet – kashrut, is one of those subjects which is generally believed to be strictly "Jewish." Most Christians would never consider that they had to regulate their diets according to YHWH's commandments. Regardless of the fact that YHWH directs our conduct in every other aspect of living, Christians seem to believe that food is somehow exempt. The notion that Believers might be prohibited from eating animals that YHWH considers detestable such as swine, bats, bottom feeding sea creatures or animals found dead on the roadside is apparently unthinkable according to current

Christian doctrine - despite the fact that these matters are specifically addressed in their Scriptures.[83]

If Christians are not supposed to observe kashrut then it seems awfully strange that many of the basics given to the Gentile converts involved dietary instructions. In fact, it is clear that the Gentile converts were expected to observe the dietary instructions found within the Torah. They were expected to live holy, set apart lives and part of living a life set apart to YHWH is eating only those things which He declared to be food and Yahushua never declared all creatures clean as some might believe.[84] There are at least 58 commandments related to food in the Torah which were not nullified by the death and resurrection of the Messiah and which Gentile converts should be observing along with their redeemed Yisraelite brethren.

The final prohibition in the Letter to the Gentile converts was to abstain from sexual immorality. The Greek word for sexual immorality is porneia (πορνεια) which means harlotry - including adultery and incest - and figuratively - idolatry. It comes from the word porneuo (πορνευο) which means to act the harlot – literally to indulge unlawful lust of either sex or figuratively to practice idolatry. The King James version of the Scriptures translates sexual immorality as fornication.

Some dictionaries define fornication as simply adultery, but it is clear from the passage that sexual immorality was referring to a variety of forms of unacceptable sexual conduct. Where might a person find out more about the prohibited conduct included in the term "sexual immorality"? The answer, of course, is in the Torah. According to my count, there are at least 24 prohibited sexual acts in Vayiqra 18 alone which would

fall under the category of sexual immorality sometimes translated as “nakedness” or ervah (ערוה) in Hebrew. Therefore, there are at least 24 additional commandments which applied to Gentile converts.

So then, the Letter to the Gentile converts instructed them to keep at least 4 categories of the Torah immediately which actually encompassed up to 135 commandments. It was assumed that they would go to the assembly on the Sabbath (which means they would also be obeying the commandments concerning the Sabbath) and learn the rest of the Torah. Why would they be instructed to go to assembly and learn Mosheh (Torah) if they were not expected to obey? The answer is obvious: The Gentile converts were expected to learn and observe the Torah along with the Hebrew Believers because they were all part of the Commonwealth of Yisrael and subject to the same Torah.

We have discussed 135 commandments which applied immediately to Gentile converts and the natural trend is that after they learned the Torah, they would obey any other commandments which they found to apply to their lives. The 10 commandments would certainly be expected to be obeyed and therefore that would have made 145 immediate commandments which should be learned. I do not like to number commandments but I am simply making a point. There was no difference between Hebrew Believers and Gentile converts concerning Torah observance. Gentile converts simply had some catching up to do.

This leads us to a Scripture passage which would seem to contradict this statement. The passage records a conversation that took place between Ya'akov and Shaul

concerning helping the four brothers complete the Nazirite vow.

Here is the conversation from a traditional modern English translation which reads: "[23] *Therefore do what we tell you: We have four men who have taken a vow.* [24] *Take them and be purified with them, and pay their expenses so that they may shave their heads, and that all may know that those things of which they were informed concerning you are nothing, but that you yourself also walk orderly and keep the law.* [25] *But concerning the Gentiles who believe, we have written and decided that they should observe no such thing, except that they should keep themselves from things offered to idols, from blood, from things strangled, and from sexual immorality.*" Acts 21:23-25 NKJV.

The New King James English translation of this passage appears to say that Gentile converts only have to obey the 4 commands but we have already seen that this was not the case at all. If you look at the Greek manuscripts from which the English translation derives you will find that many of the words are added to make it fit within the translator's preconceived theology. The underlined words were added to the English text to make it say something in English which it does not say in the Greek.

A literal translation of Acts 21:25 should read as follows: "*But concerning the Gentiles who believe, we have written and decided that they should keep themselves from what is offered to idols, and blood, and what is strangled, and whoring.*" In this passage Ya'akov was simply reiterating what had previously been determined by the Council and this corrected translation is perfectly consistent with Acts 15:20-21 which then instructs the Gentile Converts to hear and learn the Torah every Sabbath.

This example of an alteration of the text is by no means an isolated incident. While I certainly appreciate the hard work of countless translators that have given me an English translation from Hebrew and Greek manuscripts, they are by no means perfect. There are many errors that we can find in translations which need to be discovered and corrected. This does not affect the infallibility of the Word of YHWH which is not the same as ink on paper. Those that subscribe to the infallibility of a particular English translation are missing the point entirely.[85] It is critical that we identify and correct known translation errors in our search for the truth, not idolize a particular version or translation. Through this process we must be willing to change our thinking and our doctrine to align our lives with the truth of the Torah so that we may join, and embrace, the Covenant with YHWH.

11

The Torah and the Covenants

One of the primary reasons why Christianity has forsaken the Torah is because of a fundamental misunderstanding of Covenants. I believe that much of the confusion derives, in one way or another, from Dispensationalism. This doctrine has had a profound impact upon modern Christian doctrine and has helped support and establish other damaging doctrines such as Replacement Theology. So pervasive is this teaching that many are Dispensationalists without even realizing that they subscribe to the doctrine – instead they simply believe that it is an underlying truth in the Scriptures.

Dispensationalism originates from John Nelson Darby and the Plymouth Brethren in the early 1830's. In

its most recent popular form it derives primarily from the Bible School movement in the United States and the Scofield Bible. Dispensationalism tends to promote the replacement of the "old" with the "new." It teaches that the Church has replaced Yisrael and that grace has replaced the Torah, among other things. This doctrine has no

support in the Scriptures and is merely a way for men to explain the changes which have occurred within the faith over the past two thousand years.[86]

It is a very dangerous doctrine which has pervaded most of modern Christianity. I call it dangerous because it completely distorts the plan of the Creator of the Universe as described in the Scriptures and presented through His Covenants. It justifies lawlessness by advocating the abolition of the Torah and teaching that the Torah was only for the "Jews" leaving Christianity in a quandary because the Messiah - Who is the Word in flesh - obeyed the commandments and instructed those who loved Him to obey His commandments - which are not just to love one another as is commonly taught (Yahanan 14). We have already seen that He specifically stated He did not come to abolish the Torah (Mattityahu 5:17) or change it in any way.

We all have paradigms which, in essence, frame and filter the way that we perceive the world and they even control how we read the Scriptures. Christianity has certain paradigms which are reinforced through seminaries and Bible Colleges and then espoused from pulpits, through writings, television shows and radio programs. For the most part, Christianity teaches that prior to the first coming of the Messiah, man was under the Dispensation of the Law and once Yahushua "fulfilled" the Law, it was then abolished which led to the Dispensation of Grace.

Proponents of Dispensationalism basically teach that Yisrael <u>was</u> under the Dispensation of the Law while the Church <u>is</u> under the Dispensation of Grace. This is the essence of Replacement Theology, that the Church has replaced Yisrael. This leads to confusion when dealing

with prophecies relating to Yisrael which were easily explained away by declaring that the Church took the place of Yisrael. After 1948, when the modern State of Israel came into existence, it posed another problem which has again been explained away by the notion that the Church is spiritual Yisrael. None of these theological acrobatics are founded on a sound reading and interpretation of the Scriptures nor is this paradigm always presented with the label of Dispensationalism. In fact, most people receive this teaching without realizing that it is only a doctrine created by a man.

Beyond the Dispensations of Law and Grace some teach that there was also an Apostolic Dispensation where both the Law and Grace operated after the resurrection of Yahushua until the destruction of the Temple in 70 C.E. They treat the destruction of the Temple as the end of the dispensation of the Law although there is nothing in the Scriptures to substantiate this teaching nor does it even make any sense.

They do this in an attempt to explain why the Disciples of Yahushua continued to obey the Torah after His death and resurrection and to further explain why Christianity is not currently obeying the Torah. Since this is a glaring contradiction they had to find a way to make sense of this dilemma. Instead of admitting that they have been wrong and need to start obeying the commandments, they created a new dispensation.

It is important to remember that the Mishkan (Tabernacle) in

Shiloh was destroyed when the Philistines took the Ark during the time of Eli the High Priest and Shemuel. The Hekal (Temple) in Yahrushalayim had also been destroyed, abandoned and neglected on various occasions as recorded in the Tanak. None of these incidents resulted in an end of the Torah. Likewise, the destruction of the Temple in 70 C.E. did not bring about an end to the Torah. The Prophet Ezekiel even foretold of a future Hekal to be built in Yahrushalayim and the Prophets speak of a time in the future when the Sacrificial System set forth in the Torah will be reinstated.

The Torah does not rely on the existence of a physical Tabernacle or Temple here on earth nor is it affected by the absence of one. The Torah does not just include instructions regarding the Temple service - which teaches man how to worship and relate to Elohim - it also instructs the people concerning their interaction with one another. There are still Levites and Cohens whose job is to serve in the Temple and one day the Temple Service will be restored as it was in the past. These Cohens and Levites, even now, are preparing to resume their service.[87]

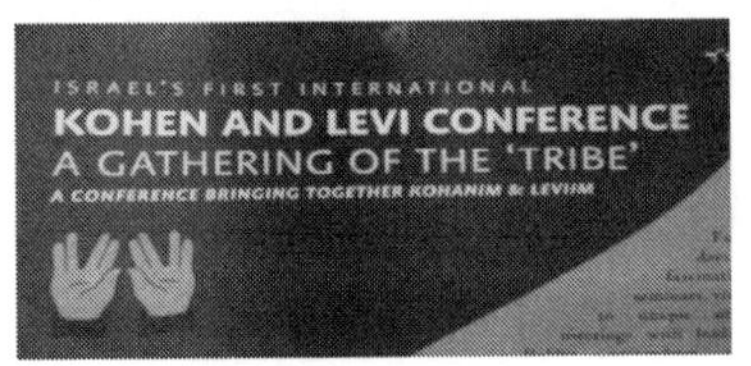

We still worship Elohim and we still interact with our fellow men on a day to day basis and therefore we still need to learn and obey the Torah. As Messiah said, "*not one jot (yud) or one tittle (stroke) of the Torah shall pass away until all is fulfilled.*" Mattityahu 5:18. If you have read the Prophets and the Book of Revelation you can easily discern that all has not been fulfilled. Therefore we still have the Torah and it is not exclusively for "Jews" - it is

for Yisrael.

By treating the Torah and grace as two diametrically opposed concepts Dispensationalists are diminishing the significance of the Torah by treating it as something temporary, obsolete and less important than grace. This teaching creates a very dangerous and confusing scenario for Christians because it places them, in some ways, in direct opposition to the plan, will and Word of YHWH. The Torah and grace are intended to operate in conjunction with one another in every Believer's life. While a person is saved by grace, they need to live their lives according to the teaching and instruction provided in the Torah.

Christianity makes frequent references to the "New" Covenant when they mention grace and the two are clearly related. The problem is that most Christians do not really know what that Covenant is or where to find it in the Scriptures. Furthermore, it is impossible to understand the so-called "New" Covenant without understanding what has been labeled the "Old" Covenant.

We read in the Scriptures that YHWH made a Covenant with the man Avram, later renamed Avraham. YHWH told him to leave the land of his father and go to a Land that would be given to his seed. Avraham was obedient to YHWH and was considered a friend of YHWH. He was promised a son through which the Covenant would be accomplished and in Beresheet 15:17 we read as YHWH passed through the cuttings of the Covenant alone - by doing so He demonstrated that He alone would fulfill the Covenant. Traditionally, both parties would pass through the cuttings as a sign that their blood would be shed if they failed to keep the covenant. By passing through the cuttings alone YHWH was taking on

the responsibility of both parties and if the Covenant was broken by either party, YHWH would bear the penalty.[88]

Through the incident on the Mount in the land of Moriah known as the Akida,[89] YHWH demonstrated how he would bear the responsibility and actually rehearsed the same scene that would be repeated by Yahushua. As Avraham and his promised son – the Scriptures emphasize his "*only son*" (Beresheet 22:2) – climb the hill in the Land, Isaac (Yitshaq)[90] carries the wood of the sacrifice on his shoulder. He willingly allows himself to be bound and laid on the altar. As Avraham was about to slaughter his promised son he is stopped and shown that YHWH provided a ram to slaughter in substitution of his son.

Through this we are shown the concept of substitution and that YHWH would provide His Son, the Lamb of Elohim, who would shed His blood to atone for our sins.[91] We are also shown how the Covenant will be fulfilled completely by YHWH and all He expects from us is faith - *which is demonstrated by obedience*.

YHWH told Avram that the whole earth would be blessed through him, but first his offspring would be strangers in captivity and they would be afflicted. We saw this come true as the Yisraelites were slaves in Mitsrayim and later delivered through Mosheh. Let's take a moment and look at Sinai because, as with Avram, it provided a pattern that will also need to be repeated. After the children of Yisrael, including the mixed multitude of

peoples, were redeemed from Mitsrayim they were then given the opportunity to enter into a marriage Covenant with YHWH. They would be the Bride and He would be their Husband. We are also given a vivid example at Sinai how the Covenant would be broken and how YHWH would renew His Covenant.

When Mosheh first ascended the mountain, YHWH cut the tablets and wrote His commandments upon them. No sooner was the Covenant made than Yisrael broke that Covenant. They constructed and worshipped an idol - the golden calf - and they did so proclaiming that it was a feast to YHWH.[92] When Mosheh saw what the people had done he broke the tablets signifying that they had broken the Covenant - they whored after other gods.

After His anger had subsided - in a demonstration of His great mercy and grace - YHWH instructed Mosheh to go back up on the mountain - only this time Mosheh was commanded to cut the stones himself and present them to YHWH. YHWH then wrote the SAME commandments on the tablets presented by man. The Covenant was not abolished or replaced, rather it was renewed.

The Covenant that was made, broken and renewed at Sinai was later renewed at Horeb before Yahushua, often called Joshua,[93] led Yisrael into the Promised Land. "[10] *All of you stand today before YHWH your Elohim: your leaders and your tribes and your elders and your officers, all the men of Yisrael,* [11] *your little ones and your wives — <u>also the stranger who is in your camp, from the one who cuts your wood to the one who draws your water</u> —* [12] *that you may enter into Covenant with YHWH your Elohim, and into His oath, which YHWH*

your Elohim makes with you today, [13] that He may establish you today as a people for Himself, and that He may be Elohim to you, just as He has spoken to you, and just as He has sworn to your fathers, to Avraham, Yitshaq, and Ya'akov. [14] 'I make this Covenant and this oath, not with you alone, [15] but with him who stands here with us today before YHWH our Elohim, as well as with him who is not here with us today.'" Devarim 29:10-15.

Just as the Sinai Covenant included the mixed multitude, the renewed Covenant at Horeb was made with non-native Yisraelites that dwelled with them. Also it was made with those who stood there that day ***as well as*** those who were not there that day. Yisrael then entered the Land and went through a period of conquering and dividing the Land amongst the tribes. At first there were no human Kings, per se, although there were Prophets, Priests and Judges who exercised authority in the Kingdom. When the people cried out for a King, YHWH answered and Shemuel anointed Shaul as King.

Shaul sinned by disobeying YHWH and the kingdom was taken from him. Thereafter Dawid was anointed as King and reigned over all of the tribes of Yisrael. Dawid proclaimed: "*Oh how I love your Torah! It is my meditation all the day.*" Tehillim 119:97. He was in love with the Torah and this is what set him apart from all other Kings of Yisrael. As a result, he reigned over a united Kingdom which extended to the reign of his son Shlomo (Solomon) although Shlomo fell away from YHWH and practiced idolatry. After the death of Shlomo, his son Rehoboam oppressed the ten northern tribes, known as

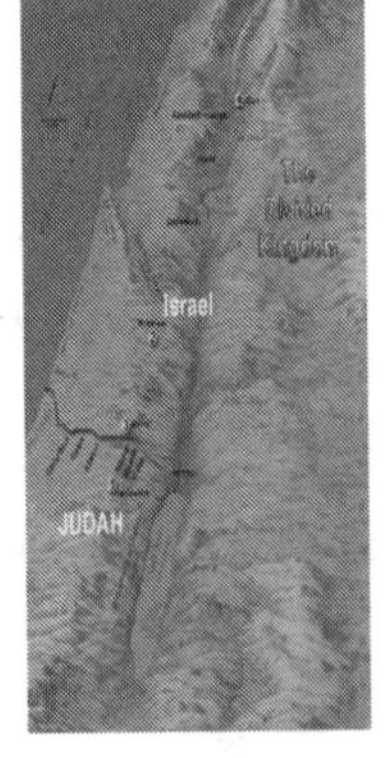

the House of Yisrael, through heavy taxation to the extent that they rebelled and broke away from the Southern Kingdom - the House of Dawid - also known as the House of Yahudah. Therefore, it was only under the reign of Dawid that the Kingdom was united under the rulership of a King who had a heart for Elohim.

After the Kingdom was divided the tribes were dealt with individually by YHWH through His Prophets. Both the Northern and Southern kingdoms fell away from YHWH and both were exiled because they disobeyed the Torah. The House of Yisrael was punished more severely because their conduct was more reprehensible. They set up the worship of two golden calves - one at Dan and one at Beth El. They did this because they had separated themselves from the Southern Kingdom - Benyamin and Yahudah – and therefore they did not go to Yahrushalayim which was geographically located within those two tribes.

The Northern Tribes committed the same sin as Yisrael did when they broke the Covenant on Sinai the first time. The House of Yisrael committed adultery and was given a divorce by YHWH.[94] As a result, these tribes were scattered to the four corners of the earth and completely lost their identity, although it was prophesied that one day they would be regathered and restored. (Hoshea 1:1-11).[95]

This regathering and restoration of the Kingdom was prophesied throughout the Tanak. The Prophet Yehezeqel (Ezekiel) gives a wonderful illustration as follows: "15 *Again the Word of YHWH came to me, saying, 16 As for you, son of man, take a stick for yourself and write on it: For Yahudah and for the children of Yisrael, his companions. Then take another stick and write on it, for Joseph, the stick of Ephraim, and for all the House of Yisrael, his companions. 17 Then join them one to another for yourself into one stick, and they will become one in your hand. 18 And when the children of your people speak to you, saying, 'Will you not show us what you mean by these?' 19 say to them, Thus says Adonai YHWH: Surely I will take the stick of Joseph, which is in the hand of Ephraim, and the tribes of Yisrael, his companions; and I will join them with it, with the stick of Yahudah, and make them one stick, and they will be one in My Hand.' 20 And the sticks on which you write will be in your hand before their eyes. 21 Then say to them, 'Thus says Adonai YHWH: Surely I will take the children of Yisrael from among the nations, wherever they have gone, and will gather them from every side and bring them into their own Land; 22 and I will make them one nation in the Land, on the mountains of Yisrael; and one king shall be king over them all; they shall no longer be two nations, nor shall they ever be divided into two kingdoms again. 23 They shall not defile themselves anymore with their idols, nor with their detestable things, nor with any of their transgressions; but I will deliver them from all their dwelling places in which they have sinned, and will cleanse them. Then they shall be My people, and I will be their Elohim. 24 Dawid My servant shall be king over them, and they shall all have one shepherd; they shall also walk in My judgments and observe My statutes, and do them. 25 Then they shall dwell in the Land that I have given to Ya'akov My servant, where your fathers dwelt; and they shall dwell there, they, their children, and their children's children, forever; and My servant Dawid shall be their prince forever. 26 Moreover I will make*

a Covenant of peace with them, and it shall be an everlasting Covenant with them; I will establish them and multiply them, and I will set My sanctuary in their midst forevermore. [27] *My Tabernacle also shall be with them; indeed I will be their Elohim, and they shall be My people.* [28] *The nations also will know that I, YHWH, sanctify Yisrael, when My sanctuary is in their midst forevermore.'"* Yehezeqel (Ezekiel) 37:15-28.

This hope of restoration was anticipated to be accomplished through the Messiah which happened, but not in a way that people anticipated. First, the House of Yisrael needed to be restored – remember she was divorced from YHWH. Both the past and future relationship between YHWH and the House of Yisrael is beautifully depicted in Hoshea 2. So then for the restoration to take place, Yisrael must be regathered and her relationship must be restored by the renewing of the Covenant – their marriage vows. This is why Yahushua commanded His talmidim to "*go to the lost sheep of the House of Yisrael.*" Mattityahu 10:6. He also stated: "*I was not sent except to the lost sheep of the House of Yisrael.*" Mattityahu 15:24. His purpose was clear and it was consistent with the promise of a renewed Covenant – not a new Covenant.

The promise of a renewed covenant to accomplish this restoration was provided by the Prophet Yirmeyahu as follows: "[31] *The time is coming, declares YHWH, when I* ***will make a renewed Covenant with the House of Yisrael and with the House of Yahudah.*** [32] *It will not be like the Covenant I made with their forefathers when I took them by the hand to lead them out of Mitsrayim, because they broke My Covenant, though I was a Husband to them, declares YHWH.* [33] *This is the Covenant I will make with the house of Yisrael after that time, declares YHWH.* ***I will put my Torah in their minds and***

write it on their hearts. I will be their Elohim, and they will be My people. *[34] No longer will a man teach his neighbor, or a man his brother, saying, know YHWH, for they shall all know Me, from the least of them to the greatest of them, declares YHWH. For I shall forgive their crookedness, and remember their sin no more.*" Yirmeyahu 31:31-34.

The essence of the Renewed Covenant is that the Torah is in our minds and written on our hearts, rather than merely words on scrolls or stone. It is all about replacing our hearts of stone with hearts of flesh as was prophesied by Yehezeqel (Ezekiel). "[22] *Therefore say to the House of Yisrael, Thus says the Adonai YHWH: I do not do this for your sake, O House of Yisrael, but for My holy Name's sake, which you have profaned among the nations wherever you went.* [23] *And I will sanctify My great Name, which has been profaned among the nations, which you have profaned in their midst; and the nations shall know that I am YHWH, says Adonai YHWH, when I am hallowed in you before their eyes.* [24] *For I will take you from among the nations, gather you out of all countries, and bring you into your own land.* [25] *Then I will sprinkle clean water on you, and you shall be clean; I will cleanse you from all your filthiness and from all your idols.* [26] *I will give you a renewed heart and put a renewed spirit within you; I will take the heart of stone out of your flesh and give you a heart of flesh.* [27] *I will put My Spirit within you and cause you to walk in My statutes, and you will keep My judgments and do them.*" Yehezeqel (Ezekiel) 36:22-28.[96]

This is what Yahushua was accomplishing while He was on the earth. He desires for us to have His Torah in our hearts and minds and to obey out of love so that we might know Him. When we ask Yahushua "into our heart" and receive salvation through faith - we are

asking the Living Word of YHWH, the Living Torah, to circumcise our hearts. When we are immersed (baptized) we are cleansing ourselves and asking YHWH to place His Spirit within us. Through this process He inscribes His Torah on our hearts and in our minds so that we may have renewed hearts to obey Him and begin to live righteous, set apart lives. This is the Renewed Covenant and it is all about the Torah.

The Renewed Covenant is made between YHWH and the House of Yisrael and the House of Yahudah. The Renewed Covenant is not made with a new and distinct organization called the Christian Church or the Body of Christ. The Covenant is renewed with the same ones that received the former Covenant - Yisrael. Just as Yisrael consisted of a mixed multitude when they were delivered from Mitsrayim, so the Yisrael of today, which constitutes the set apart assembly, is a mixed multitude of people - not necessarily all genetic descendants of Avraham, Yitshaq and Ya'akov - but very likely many are indeed.

They are scattered around the world and have been mixed with the nations, but the Messiah will gather His sheep. The Scriptures even record how this will be accomplished: "[14] *Therefore behold, the days are coming, says YHWH, that it shall no more be said, 'YHWH lives who brought up the children of Yisrael from the land of Mitsrayim,'* [15] *but, 'YHWH lives who brought up the children of Yisrael from the land of the north and from all the lands where He had driven them.'* *<u>For I will bring them back into their Land which I gave to their fathers.</u>* [16] *<u>Behold, I will send for many fishermen, says YHWH, and they shall fish them; and afterward I will send for many hunters, and they shall hunt them</u> from every mountain and every hill, and out of the holes of the rocks.*" Yirmeyahu

16:14-17.

Yahushua called His disciples "*fishers of men*" for this very reason. (Mattityahu 4:19; Mark 1:17). Sadly, most "Jews" have not recognized the Messiah because they believe that He failed to unite the tribes and restore the Kingdom. This is exactly what He came to do but Christianity has failed to understand and teach the big picture. As a result, they have obscured the work of Messiah. They have focused so much on Jesus being a "personal savior" and "building His Church" that they missed a fundamental objective of His ministry which involves gathering the outcasts and the restoration of Yisrael – both through His first and second coming.

Thus the notion that the Church has replaced Yisrael is a failure to understand the Covenants. Nothing can replace Yisrael, but you must understand that Yisrael consists of those whose hearts have been circumcised, not merely genetic descendents of the twelve tribes of Yisrael. If you are part of the family of Elohim you must take hold of the Covenant and join with Yisrael – The Olive Tree.[97]

This is what Shaul meant by being "grafted in" to Yisrael (Romans 11). The Olive Tree of Yisrael consists of both wild and natural branches. The natural branches are broken off because of unbelief and wild branches are grafted in because of belief. We are not talking about the modern State of Israel, which currently occupies a small portion of the Covenant Land, but rather the Yisrael of Elohim. (Galatians 6:16).

Shaul's analogy of the Olive Tree is pure Torah teaching regarding the native-born Yisraelite (natural branch) and the sojourner (wild branch) and how one enters into the Covenant. If a native-born Yisraelite refused to follow Torah they were cut off from the Covenant. If a sojourner desired to follow YHWH then they needed to follow Torah and they would be treated the same as a native-born – grafted into the Covenant. Thus Yisrael consisted of everyone who dwelled in the camp, or in the Land, who followed Torah and lived in obedience to the instructions – both the native-born and the sojourner.

When Shaul stated that "*all Yisrael would be saved*" (Romans 11:26) he was not making a blanket statement that every "Jew" or all genetic descendents of the twelve tribes would supernaturally be saved at some point in the future. Rather, he was referring to all those who are the Seed of Avraham (Galatians 3:29), who share the belief and faith of Avraham - every one who is grafted into the tree is Yisrael. Thus, when the time is right - all who belong to Yisrael will be saved according to the Covenant. (Yeshayahu 27:9; Yirmeyahu 31:33).

We can plainly see from the ministry of the Messiah the marriage language that He uses which emphasizes the purpose of His ministry. He sat at the Last Supper with twelve representatives of the Tribes of Yisrael – symbolic of His united Kingdom – His Bride. In ancient Eastern culture, that meal was the traditional meal which would occur when a Bride and a Bridegroom agree on the terms of the marriage. It seals the agreement (covenant) wherein the bridegroom then departs to "prepare a place" for His bride. While the bridegroom is away, the bride prepares herself, she cleanses herself, keeps herself pure "without

spot or blemish" and learns the ways of her husband. The groom would typically go prepare a place for himself and his bride by building onto his father's house and when the marriage home was ready the bridegroom then returned "*as a thief in the night*" to claim his bride. They then had a feast and consummated the relationship.

Yisrael is the Bride that Yahushua will be returning to claim – not the Church - and this Bride will include all of those who believe and are ready. If you are part of Yisrael then you are in the Covenant and the Torah is an integral part of that Covenant. You cannot have one without the other. Likewise, the Land is also a significant part of the Covenant which many Christians fail to recognize. They believe that the Land Covenant is separate from the other Covenants – it is not. When Messiah returns, His Bride will not be floating on clouds strumming harps – she will be in the Promised Land with Her Husband.

Thus the Renewed Covenant was consummated by Yahushua at what is commonly referred to as "The Last Supper." "*In the same way, after the supper He took the cup, saying, 'This cup is the renewed Covenant in My blood, which is poured out for you.'*" Luke 22:20. Many modern translations state: "*this cup is the new Covenant*" which is an incorrect translation. The word translated as "new" is kainee (καινη) which means: "refreshed or renewed." If the intent was to invoke a brand new Covenant the word neo (νεο) would have likely been used.

This interpretation is completely consistent with the language used by Yirmeyahu, Yeshayahu and Yehezeqel. In Hebrew the word for renew is hadashah (חדשה) and the word for covenant is brit (ברית). Thus the Renewed Covenant is referred to as the Brit Hadashah.

YHWH gives us a wonderful example of renewal through His creation. Despite the fact that much of the world reckons time according to a solar calendar, the Scriptural calendar revolves around the sun and the moon.[98] Months begin at the sighting of the "new moon" which is referred to as hodesh (חדש).

We know when we see the "new moon" that it is really not a brand new moon which appears approximately every 28 days. The number of days in a cycle depends upon whether you are measuring according to the synodic cycle (29.5 days) or the sidereal cycle (27.1 days) thus the average is 28 days. Therefore, it is a renewed moon or a refreshed moon. Notice the similarity between the words hadashah (חדשה) and hodesh (חדש). They share the same root meaning of renewal and the only difference is the hey (ה).[99] Therefore, just as the moon is refreshed in its time so the Covenant is refreshed in YHWH's time.

Yahushua was the mediator of the Renewed Covenant just as Mosheh was the mediator of the Sinai Covenant. Of course we were provided with this pattern when Mosheh renewed the Covenant at Moab and when Yahushua (Joshua) renewed the Covenant at Shechem. Notice that there were no Gentiles at the table during the Last Supper, there were only Yisraelites. Not all twelve tribes were present at the table, but they were clearly represented, just as was done during the rededication of the Temple by Nehemyah and Ezra. (Ezra 6:17). Therefore, the Renewed Covenant was prophesied to Yisrael and it was made with Yisrael. The notion that YHWH is somehow finished with Yisrael is absurd, because if He is

done with Yisrael then the Covenant is ended and there are no promises for us to rely upon for redemption.

History shows us that the Christian religion has attempted to hijack the Renewed Covenant and somehow replace Yisrael, but the Christian Church was never a party to any Covenant. You cannot separate Yisrael from the Renewed Covenant because without Yisrael there is no Renewed Covenant. Shaul clearly stated: "[4] *the people of Yisrael. Theirs is the adoption as sons; theirs the divine glory, the Covenants, the receiving of the Torah, the Temple worship and the promises.* [5] *Theirs are the patriarchs, and from them is traced the human ancestry of Messiah, who is Elohim over all, forever praised! Amen.*" Romans 9:3-5. The promises and the Covenants belong to Yisrael – if you want them you must join Yisrael.

This is why we see so many Christians suffering from an identity crisis. There are literally hundreds of denominations, sects and cults - all with differing rules, regulations, hierarchies and beliefs from the others - each one believing that they have the "full gospel." They do not even know how to deal with each other – let alone Yisrael. Most all of them removed the Torah from their tents and sprinkled what little truth was left with grace to the point where what Christians perceive as the Renewed Covenant is something very different from that described by Mosheh and the Prophets.

Gentiles only enter into the Renewed Covenant through Yisrael and simply put - if you have been taught anything different - you have been taught a lie. If you recognize this truth then you may actually see the fulfillment of prophecy occur in your life. The Prophet Yirmeyahu immediately after prophesying concerning the

fishers and the hunters stated: "[19] . . . *the Gentiles shall come to you from the ends of the earth and say, 'Surely our fathers have inherited lies, worthlessness and unprofitable things.* [20] *Will a man make gods for himself, which are not gods?* [21] *Therefore behold, I will this once cause them to know, I will cause them to know My hand and My might; and they shall know that My Name is YHWH.'"* Yirmeyahu 16:19-21.

I grew up in the Christian faith and there came a point in my life when I realized that I had been lied to and I had to undergo a complete paradigm shift. I personally experienced the prophecy given by Yirmeyahu and I discovered the Name of YHWH which had been hidden from me most of my life. I realized that I had to enter into the Covenant and I experienced another prophecy from the Prophet Yeshayahu concerning salvation of the Gentiles.

"[1] *Thus says YHWH: Keep justice, and do righteousness, for My salvation is about to come, and My righteousness to be revealed.* [2] *Blessed is the man who does this, and the son of man who lays hold on it; who keeps from defiling the Sabbath, and keeps his hand from doing any evil.* [3] *Do not let the son of the foreigner who has joined himself to YHWH speak, saying, YHWH has utterly separated me from His people; nor let the eunuch say, Here I am, a dry tree.* [4] *For thus says YHWH: To the eunuchs who keep My Sabbaths, and choose what pleases Me, and hold fast My Covenant,* [5] *Even to them I will give in My House and within My walls a place and a name better than that of sons and daughters; I will give them an everlasting name that shall not be cut off.* [6] *Also the sons of the foreigner who join themselves to YHWH, to serve Him, and to love the Name of YHWH, to be His servants — Everyone who keeps from defiling the Sabbath, and holds fast My Covenant —* [7] *Even*

them I will bring to My holy mountain, and make them joyful in My House of Prayer. Their burnt offerings and their sacrifices will be accepted on My Altar; for My House shall be called a House of Prayer for all nations. [8] ***Adonai YHWH, who gathers the outcasts of Yisrael, says, Yet I will gather to him others besides those who are gathered to him.***" Yeshayahu 56:1-8.

Keeping justice and doing righteousness refers specifically to the Torah. Notice that the Gentiles are told to "*lay hold,*" "*join themselves*" and "*hold fast*" to the Covenant. This gives the impression that someone is trying to take it away from them - which is exactly what is happening today. As Gentiles are returning to the truth and taking hold of the Covenant they are being told by Christians that they are putting themselves "under the law" and they are being told by some "Jews" that they cannot obey the Torah.[100] They are being challenged and discouraged from all sides - that is why they are given these encouraging words from the Prophet. No matter what happens - do not let anyone make you think or believe that "*YHWH has utterly separated [you] from His people.*"

If you have entered the Renewed Covenant through Yahushua – the Way, the Truth, the Life and the Light – then you have entered in through the Living Torah and you are in the Commonwealth of Yisrael. He will give you a name better than sons and daughters and you have a place in His House and the rule of His House is the Torah.

12

Grace

Up to this point I have alluded to grace without having actually defined the word. This was done intentionally in order to establish the significance of the Torah before examining the use and misuse of the doctrine of grace. All too often the Torah has been swept aside by some twisted understanding of grace which has been stretched far beyond its intended meaning.

The English word "grace" derives from the Latin "gratia" which means "gratitude" or "thanks." This is illustrated in the Spanish phrase "muchas gracias" which means: "much thanks." When people say grace prior to eating a meal they are supposed to be giving thanks for the food although some people "give the blessing" which apparently insures that the food will be edible regardless of whether it is actually food as defined by the Scriptures.

Yahushua was only recorded as using the word "grace" four times and then, only in the Book of Luke. In each instance it is used in the context of thanks. Nowhere does Yahushua allude to the notion that the Grace of YHWH would work to abolish His Torah. Sadly this is what is taught and believed throughout much of Christianity.

In fact, Christianity has developed an entire

doctrine around the word grace so it may be helpful to take a moment and examine the source of this misplaced understanding. Most Christians know the Scripture passage: "*For it is by grace you have been saved, through faith - and this not from yourselves, it is the gift of Elohim.*" Ephesians 2:8. What does this mean? Simply put, it shows that but for the grace of YHWH, we would not be saved.

Grace is a conduit for salvation. It is a gift that is freely given so that no man would boast that he somehow earned his salvation (Ephesians 2:9). No man is perfect therefore no man can be saved outside of the grace of YHWH. The problem arises when people start treating grace as something new and mutually exclusive from the Torah. They believe that the two are adversarial and that grace has somehow won the struggle and replaced the Torah.

The Greek word which is translated as "grace" in the English language is χαριν (charis). χαριν (charis) is where we derive such words as "charisma" and "charity" and it is generally associated with charm or beauty. In Hellenistic cultures these words were associated and personified through goddesses commonly referred to as "The Hours" or the "Three Graces." They are also known as The Charities according to the Wikipedia encyclopedia: In Greek mythology, a Charis is one of several Charites (Χάριτες; Greek: 'Graces'), goddesses of charm, beauty, nature, human creativity and fertility. They ordinarily numbered three, from youngest to oldest: Aglaea (Beauty), Euphrosyne (Mirth), and Thalia (Good Cheer). In Roman mythology they were known as the Gratiae."

The Hebrew word which is often translated in English Bibles as "grace" is חן (hen). חן (hen) means "beauty," "loveliness," "elegance" and can also mean "favor." It does not fully encompass the common Christian usage of the word. Another Hebrew word which also reflects the Christian understanding of "grace" is חשד (hesed) which means "goodness" or "kindness" although it is usually translated into English as "mercy."

It is plain to see that the English word "grace" has diverse origins and usage and the original context of the Hebrew Scriptures has not necessarily been properly represented by using the word "grace" in the English language. This can lead some to believe that there was little to no "grace" found in the Hebrew Scriptures (Tanak) when, in fact, חשד (hesed) is found 274 times while חן (hen) is found 69 times. There are also numerous other Hebrew words which involve the concepts of "mercy," "compassion," "patience," "goodness," "favor" and "kindness" all which are elements included within the Christian concept of "grace."

> Nelson's Bible Dictionary defines grace as: "Favor or kindness shown without regard to the worth or merit of the one who receives it and in spite of what that same person deserves. Grace is one of the key attributes of [Elohim]. [YHWH Elohim] is 'merciful and gracious, long-suffering, and abounding in goodness and truth' (Shemot 34:6). Therefore, grace is almost always associated with mercy, love, compassion, and patience as the source of help and with deliverance from distress.

> In the [Tanak], a prime example of grace was the redemption of the Hebrew people from Egypt and their establishment in the Promised Land. This did not happen because of any merit on Israel's part, but in spite of their unrighteousness (Devarim 9:5-6). Although the grace of [Elohim] is always free and undeserved, it must not be taken for granted. Grace is only enjoyed within the Covenant - the gift is given by [Elohim], and the gift is received by man through repentance and faith (Amos 5:15). Grace is to be humbly sought through the prayer of faith (Malachi 1:9). The grace of [Elohim] was supremely revealed and given in the person and work of [Yahushua Messiah]. [Yahushua] was not only the beneficiary of [Elohim's] grace (Luke 2:40), but He was also its very embodiment (Yahanan 1:14), bringing it to mankind for salvation (Titus 2:11). By His death and resurrection, [Yahushua] restored the broken fellowship between Elohim and His people, both Jew and Gentile.[101]

Obviously this is not the same meaning as the etymology provides although it is a reasonably thorough and accurate definition of the concept which grace was meant to express. Sadly, not all Christian Bible Commentaries are so precise. Read the following definition of grace from another commentary:

> GRACE - salvation by grace in the New

Testament is opposed to an Old Testament doctrine of salvation by works (Romans 4:4; 11:6), or, what is the same thing, by law.[102]

Regretably, this comment is absolutely false - Yisrael was never saved by their obedience to the Torah. While it was considered righteousness for them to observe the Torah (Devarim 6:25) they were never justified by their works. In fact, as previously mentioned, the Sacrificial system outlined in the Torah only provided atonement for unintentional sin - there is no specified sacrifice for intentional sin outside of the mercy of YHWH.

Interestingly, when we are provided with this information in the Scriptures we are told that the Torah is the same for a native born as it is for a stranger who dwells in the assembly. "[14] *And if a stranger dwells with you, or whoever is among you throughout your generations, and would present an offering made by fire, a sweet aroma to YHWH, **just as you do, so shall he do**.* [15] *One ordinance shall be for you of the assembly and for the stranger who dwells with you, an ordinance forever throughout your generations; as you are, so shall the stranger be before YHWH.* [16] ***One Torah and one custom shall be for you and for the stranger who dwells with you.***" Bemidbar 15:14-16.

A little further in the same portion of Scripture we are told: "*You shall have one Torah for him who sins unintentionally, for him who is native-born among the children of Yisrael and for the stranger who dwells among them.*" Bemidbar 15:29.

Thus it was always understood that the Torah was for all people who desired to dwell with YHWH. Obedience to the Torah did not bring about salvation

because there was the unresolved issue of intentional sin which leads to death. It was also understood that we needed the unmerited favor – hesed – of YHWH to live – which is commonly referred to as grace.

It is through the favor of YHWH that we are offered the free gift of life everlasting. This unmerited favor resulted from something that YHWH did – there was nothing we could do to earn it. Just as He put Avram asleep when the Covenant was made and just as He showed that He would provide the ram – He is the One who would do it all.

There is nothing that Torah observance can do to earn that gift. What is required is the same faith that Avraham demonstrated. We need to believe the promises of YHWH – the promises which He provided through His Covenant – and we need to demonstrate our belief through our actions. "*For as the body without the spirit is dead, so faith without works is dead also.*" Ya'akov 2:26.

The question that remains is: What do we do once we receive the gift and enter into the Renewed Covenant? Our response, as we have already seen, should then be obedience to Torah. You see, grace and Torah operate together in perfect harmony. The Torah shows us that we need favor and once we receive the gift freely given we should naturally walk in the ways of the Torah as an expression of our love and appreciation.

Sadly the paradigm that the Torah and grace are opposed to one another has been perpetuated by countless books, sermons and commentaries as well as erroneous Scriptural translations.

Grace is not some new concept introduced in the Messianic Scriptures – it is evident from the beginning

of creation. The fact that man was created and given the breath of life is the ultimate act of favour and kindness provided by the Creator. He then gave man dominion over creation - again grace. In fact, once you shift your inherited paradigm you will find grace throughout the Tanak.

It is evident from the lives of such men as Noah and Avraham. They believed in the promises of YHWH. They put their faith and trust in YHWH - their faith was counted toward righteousness - and their obedience led to their being blessed. The Scriptures record that: "*Noah found grace in the eyes of YHWH*" (Beresheet 6:8) and his obedience led to the deliverance and salvation of mankind. He believed YHWH <u>and</u> he acted upon the instructions which saved him and his family from judgment. Could it be any clearer?

Avraham's faith was counted toward righteousness and he is renowned for his life of obedience. (Beresheet 15:6). The Scriptures also record that Yisrael's observance of YHWH's commands and their fear of YHWH was accounted as righteousness to them; both of which signal faith and belief. "[24] *And YHWH commanded us to observe all these statutes, to fear YHWH our Elohim, for our good always, that He might preserve us alive, as it is this day.*[25] *Then it will be righteousness for us, if we are careful to observe all these commandments before YHWH our Elohim, as He has commanded us.*" Devarim 6:24-25.

Mosheh viewed grace as a sort of prerequisite for knowing the Ways of YHWH which allowed him to know the Almighty. "[13] *Now therefore, I pray, <u>if I have found grace in Your sight, show me now Your way, that I may know You and that I may find grace in Your sight</u>. And consider that*

this nation is Your people. [14] *And He said, 'My Presence will go with you, and I will give you rest.'"* Shemot 33:13-14.

This should be our yearning as well. Mosheh asked for grace and he received the Presence of YHWH and His rest. We read also: "[8] *So Mosheh made haste and bowed his head toward the earth, and worshiped.* [9] *Then he said, 'If now I have found grace in Your sight, O Adonai, let my Adonai, I pray, go among us, even though we are a stiff-necked people; and pardon our iniquity and our sin, and take us as Your inheritance.'"* Shemot 34:8-9.

Encapsulated in these requests is what every person should desire because this is what the Messiah accomplished. He came with the Truth of Torah as well as grace which allows us to enter into the Renewed Covenant. Through the work of Messiah we have the Spirit and we have rest, our sins are forgiven and YHWH has taken us as His inheritance.

Sadly, grace has been treated as something diametrically opposed to the Torah which is a grievous mistake. Without the Torah as a foundation, grace has become a license to sin for many. The Torah provided the framework within which mankind was intended to live. The word garden in Hebrew is gan (גן) which specifically refers to a place which is fenced in or hedged about. Thus when mankind lived in the garden he was living within the boundaries of the Torah.

Since the transgression in the gard expulsion of Adam and Hawah, we all need favor to restore us into right relationship with our Creator. Thus - grace is the starting point of our journey of restoration. It reopens the entrance to the garden which

was once closed to mankind. It is because of grace that we can become cleansed from our sins and endeavor upon a life of obedience to the Torah, not the other way around.

The Torah shows us how to walk and be blessed through the favor of Elohim, but many miss those blessings because they are walking outside of the protective hedge of the garden - outside of the Torah - outside of the Covenant.

13

Blessings and Curses

The Scriptures, in a large part, detail the desire of YHWH to find a people who will be obedient to His Ways and dwell with Him forever. It is His desire and requirement that those in His House respect and obey His rules. Those who carry His Name are subject to His instructions just as any child obeys his or her parents.

The rules of my house do not define the relationship with my children. My daughter is my daughter no matter what and my son is still my son no matter what. Nothing will change the fact that I love them immensely and nothing would ever change the fact that they are my children. That having been said, if they simply refuse to obey the rules of my house - we are going to have a problem. If they refuse to obey my rules and try to bring filthy, repulsive or abominable things into my home it will not be tolerated. Disobedience to the rules of my home will result in punishment.

We are provided with these tangible relationships so that we can better understand our Creator. This practical example should help us better understand how we should view the Torah. It is not just a bunch of do's

and don'ts meant to make our lives miserable or put us into bondage. Rather the goal is to get us in line with the will of our perfect and holy Heavenly Father so that we can dwell with Him in abundance and peace.

The Scriptures are filled with the promise of blessings which follow obedience although they never state that obedience brings salvation and, as mentoned previously, Yisrael was never saved through obedience to the Torah. While the Torah made provision for the atonement of an unintentional violation of the Torah through the slaughter of certain animals, those sacrifices could never provide atonement for willful disobedience. (Bemidbar 15:29-31).

Intentional sin required death of the offender and forgiveness for willful defiant disobedience required a greater slaughter offering which only a Redeemer can provide. Therefore, obedience was always associated with promises of blessings, not salvation, although salvation is connected to the Torah in that a person who is saved should also be obedient to the Torah. How can you truly demonstrate belief when you refuse to obey the instructions of the One Who saved you? Will you accept His free gift and then reject His ways? Notice the nexus: "*Salvation is far from the wicked, for they do not seek Your statutes.*" Tehillim 119:155 NKJV. The wicked are always those who disobey the Truth.

In contrast, some modern day sects of Christianity incorrectly teach that faith produces the blessing. The teaching generally leads people to believe that if they can muster enough faith they will be healed, they will experience abundance, prosperity etc. The problem is that they treat faith as some ethereal concept without definition

or substance.

The Scriptures define faith as: "[1] . . . *the substance of things hoped for, the evidence of things not seen . . .* [3] *By faith we understand that the worlds were framed by the Word of Elohim, so that the things which are seen were not made of things which are visible.*" Ibrim 11:1-3. Our faith must come from a belief in our Elohim and the promises which He has made to us through His Word. Those promises are found within the Torah and the Prophets. YHWH promises many blessings if we obey and therefore our obedience is an exercise in faith which brings about those blessings. When we act upon those promises it makes our faith evident and tangible because we are able to witness the results of our faith. Any other means of conjuring up faith is contrary to the Scriptures.

The Scriptures specifically warn us: "[32] . . . *be careful to do what YHWH your Elohim has commanded you; do not turn aside to the right or to the left.* [33] *Walk in all the way that YHWH your Elohim has commanded you,* ***so that you may live and prosper and prolong your days in the Land that you will possess.***" Devarim 5:32-33. These promises are extended to the Gentiles who turn to YHWH and join the Covenant. (Yeshayahu 56:4-6).

"[24] *And YHWH commanded us to obey all these decrees and to fear YHWH our Elohim,* ***for our good always, to keep us alive,*** *as it is today.* [25] *And it is righteousness for us when we guard to do all this command before YHWH our Elohim, as He has commanded us.*" Devarim 6:24-25. Notice that it is for our own good that we obey the commands and that it is righteousness to guard (shamar) and to do the commands of YHWH. "*In this the children of Elohim and the children of the devil are manifest: Whoever does not practice*

righteousness is not of Elohim, nor is he who does not love his brother." 1 Yahanan 3:10. Likewise, whoever does practice righteousness by obeying the commandments is a child of Elohim, this is how they manifest themselves.

Obedience also has many further blessings – here are some Scriptures which detail them. "[5] *Now therefore, if you will indeed obey My voice and keep My Covenant, then* ***you shall be a special treasure to Me above all people; for all the earth is Mine.*** [6] ***And you shall be to Me a kingdom of priests and a holy nation.*** *These are the words which you shall speak to the children of Yisrael.*" Shemot 19:5-6.

"[17] *Diligently guard (shamar) the commands of YHWH your Elohim, and His testimonies, and His statutes which He has commanded you.* [18] *And you shall do what is right and good in the eyes of YHWH, that* ***it might be well with you, and you shall go in and possess the good Land of which YHWH swore to your fathers,*** [19] ***to drive out all our enemies from before you, as YHWH has spoken.***" Devarim 6:17-19.

"[8] *This Scroll of the Torah shall not depart from your mouth, but you shall meditate in it day and night, that you may observe to do according to all that is written in it. For then* ***you will make your way prosperous, and then you will have good success.*** [9] *Have I not commanded you? Be strong and of good courage; do not be afraid, nor be dismayed, for YHWH your Elohim is with you wherever you go.*" Yahushua 1:8-9.

"[1] *Blessed is the man who walks not in the counsel of the ungodly, nor stands in the path of sinners, nor sits in the seat of the scornful;* [2] *But his delight is in the Torah of YHWH, and in His Torah he meditates day and night.*" Tehillim 1:1-2.

Devarim 28 specifically details the blessings that follow obedience:

> [1] *Now it shall come to pass, if you*

diligently obey the voice of YHWH your Elohim,
to observe carefully all His commandments
which I command you today, that YHWH
your Elohim will set you high above all nations
of the earth.[2] And all these blessings shall come
upon you and overtake you, because you obey
the voice of YHWH your Elohim: [3] Blessed
shall you be in the city, and blessed shall you
be in the country. [4] Blessed shall be the fruit
of your body, the produce of your ground and
the increase of your herds, the increase of your
cattle and the offspring of your flocks. [5] Blessed
shall be your basket and your kneading bowl.
[6] Blessed shall you be when you come in, and
blessed shall you be when you go out. [7] YHWH
will cause your enemies who rise against you to
be defeated before your face; they shall come out
against you one way and flee before you seven
ways. [8] YHWH will command the blessing on
you in your storehouses and in all to which you
set your hand, and He will bless you in the land
which YHWH your Elohim is giving you. [9]
YHWH will establish you as a holy people to
Himself, just as He has sworn to you, if you
keep (shamar) the commandments of YHWH
your Elohim and walk in His ways.[10] Then
all peoples of the earth shall see that you are
called by the name of YHWH, and they shall
be afraid of you.[11] And YHWH will grant you
plenty of goods, in the fruit of your body, in the
increase of your livestock, and in the produce
of your ground, in the Land of which YHWH

swore to your fathers to give you.[12] *YHWH will open to you His good treasure, the heavens, to give the rain to your Land in its season, and to bless all the work of your hand. You shall lend to many nations, but you shall not borrow.*[13] *And YHWH will make you the head and not the tail; you shall be above only, and not be beneath, if you heed the commandments of YHWH your Elohim, which I command you today, and are careful to observe (shamar) them.*[14] *So you shall not turn aside from any of the words which I command you this day, to the right or the left, to go after other gods to serve them."* Devarim 28:1-14.

The confusion in Christianity begins with the mistaken belief that since these promises were from the "Old Testament" that they were meant only for "the Jews." The Christian belief is that "the Jews" were under the Torah while Christians are under grace. Due to this thinking the majority of Christendom believes that they do not have to obey the Torah of YHWH. As a result, many end up living in a state of disobedience which leads to their not only missing the blessing, but also potentially falling under a curse. Christians like to talk about, hear about, read about and claim the blessings found in the Scriptures, but they fail to realize that there are often conditions to receiving a blessing. The same holds true for receiving a curse.

"[26] *Behold, I set before you today a blessing and a curse:* [27] *the blessing, if you obey the commandments of YHWH your Elohim which I command you today;* [28] *and the curse, if you do not obey the commandments of YHWH your Elohim, but turn*

aside from the way which I command you today, to go after other gods which you have not known." Devarim 11:26-29.

The curses are also clearly described in Scripture as follows:

> [15]*But it shall come to pass, if you do not obey the voice of YHWH your Elohim, to observe carefully all His commandments and His statutes which I command you today, that all these curses will come upon you and overtake you:* [16] *Cursed shall you be in the city, and cursed shall you be in the country.* [17] *Cursed shall be your basket and your kneading bowl.* [18] *Cursed shall be the fruit of your body and the produce of your land, the increase of your cattle and the offspring of your flocks.*[19] *Cursed shall you be when you come in, and cursed shall you be when you go out.* [20] *YHWH will send on you cursing, confusion, and rebuke in all that you set your hand to do, until you are destroyed and until you perish quickly, because of the wickedness of your doings in which you have forsaken Me.*[21] *YHWH will make the plague cling to you until He has consumed you from the Land which you are going to possess.* [22] *YHWH will strike you with consumption, with fever, with inflammation, with severe burning fever, with the sword, with scorching, and with mildew; they shall pursue you until you perish.* [23] *And your heavens which are over your head shall be bronze, and the earth which is under you shall be iron.* [24] *YHWH will change the rain of your Land to powder and dust; from the heaven it shall come down on you*

until you are destroyed. 25 YHWH will cause
you to be defeated before your enemies; you shall
go out one way against them and flee seven ways
before them; and you shall become troublesome
to all the kingdoms of the earth. 26 Your carcasses
shall be food for all the birds of the air and the
beasts of the earth, and no one shall frighten
them away. 27 YHWH will strike you with the
boils of Mitsrayim, with tumors, with the scab,
and with the itch, from which you cannot be
healed. 28 YHWH will strike you with madness
and blindness and confusion of heart. 29 And you
shall grope at noonday, as a blind man gropes in
darkness; you shall not prosper in your ways;
you shall be only oppressed and plundered
continually, and no one shall save you. 30 You
shall betroth a wife, but another man shall lie
with her; you shall build a house, but you shall
not dwell in it; you shall plant a vineyard, but
shall not gather its grapes. 31 Your ox shall be
slaughtered before your eyes, but you shall not
eat of it; your donkey shall be violently taken
away from before you, and shall not be restored
to you; your sheep shall be given to your enemies,
and you shall have no one to rescue them. 32 Your
sons and your daughters shall be given to another
people, and your eyes shall look and fail with
longing for them all day long; and there shall be
no strength in your hand. 33 A nation whom you
have not known shall eat the fruit of your land
and the produce of your labor, and you shall be
only oppressed and crushed continually. 34 So

you shall be driven mad because of the sight
which your eyes see. [35] YHWH will strike you
in the knees and on the legs with severe boils
which cannot be healed, and from the sole of
your foot to the top of your head. [36] YHWH will
bring you and the king whom you set over you to
a nation which neither you nor your fathers have
known, and there you shall serve other gods -
wood and stone. [37] And you shall become an
astonishment, a proverb, and a byword among
all nations where YHWH will drive you. [38]
You shall carry much seed out to the field but
gather little in, for the locust shall consume it. [39]
You shall plant vineyards and tend them, but
you shall neither drink of the wine nor gather
the grapes; for the worms shall eat them. [40] You
shall have olive trees throughout all your
territory, but you shall not anoint yourself with
the oil; for your olives shall drop off. [41] You shall
beget sons and daughters, but they shall not be
yours; for they shall go into captivity. [42] Locusts
shall consume all your trees and the produce of
your land. [43] The alien who is among you shall
rise higher and higher above you, and you shall
come down lower and lower.[44] He shall lend to
you, but you shall not lend to him; he shall be the
head, and you shall be the tail. [45] Moreover all
these curses shall come upon you and pursue and
overtake you, until you are destroyed, because
you did not obey the voice of YHWH your
Elohim, to keep (shamar) His commandments
and His statutes which He commanded you.[46]

*And they shall be upon you for a sign and a
wonder, and on your descendants forever.* 47
*Because you did not serve YHWH your Elohim
with joy and gladness of heart, for the abundance
of everything,* 48 *therefore you shall serve your
enemies, whom YHWH will send against you,
in hunger, in thirst, in nakedness, and in need of
everything; and He will put a yoke of iron on
your neck until He has destroyed you.* 49 *YHWH
will bring a nation against you from afar, from
the end of the earth, as swift as the eagle flies, a
nation whose language you will not understand,* 50
*a nation of fierce countenance, which does not
respect the elderly nor show favor to the young.* 51
*And they shall eat the increase of your livestock
and the produce of your land, until you are
destroyed; they shall not leave you grain or new
wine or oil, or the increase of your cattle or the
offspring of your flocks, until they have destroyed
you.* 52 *They shall besiege you at all your gates
until your high and fortified walls, in which you
trust, come down throughout all your land; and
they shall besiege you at all your gates throughout
all your land which YHWH your Elohim has
given you.* 53 *You shall eat the fruit of your own
body, the flesh of your sons and your daughters
whom YHWH your Elohim has given you, in
the siege and desperate straits in which your
enemy shall distress you.* 54 *The sensitive and
very refined man among you will be hostile
toward his brother, toward the wife of his bosom,
and toward the rest of his children whom he*

leaves behind,[55] so that he will not give any of them the flesh of his children whom he will eat, because he has nothing left in the siege and desperate straits in which your enemy shall distress you at all your gates.[56] The tender and delicate woman among you, who would not venture to set the sole of her foot on the ground because of her delicateness and sensitivity, will refuse to the husband of her bosom, and to her son and her daughter,[57] her placenta which comes out from between her feet and her children whom she bears; for she will eat them secretly for lack of everything in the siege and desperate straits in which your enemy shall distress you at all your gates. [58] If you do not carefully observe (shamar) all the words of this Torah that are written in this book, that you may fear this glorious and awesome Name, YHWH your Elohim, [59] then YHWH will bring upon you and your descendants extraordinary plagues - great and prolonged plagues - and serious and prolonged sicknesses.[60] Moreover He will bring back on you all the diseases of Mitsrayim, of which you were afraid, and they shall cling to you· [61] Also every sickness and every plague, which is not written in this Scroll of the Torah, will YHWH bring upon you until you are destroyed.[62] You shall be left few in number, whereas you were as the stars of heaven in multitude, because you would not obey the voice of YHWH your Elohim. [63] And it shall be, that just as YHWH rejoiced over you to do you good and multiply

you, so YHWH will rejoice over you to destroy you and bring you to nothing; and you shall be plucked from off the land which you go to possess.
[64] Then YHWH will scatter you among all peoples, from one end of the earth to the other, and there you shall serve other gods, which neither you nor your fathers have known - wood and stone.[65] And among those nations you shall find no rest, nor shall the sole of your foot have a resting place; but there YHWH will give you a trembling heart, failing eyes, and anguish of soul.[66] Your life shall hang in doubt before you; you shall fear day and night, and have no assurance of life.[67] In the morning you shall say, Oh, that it were evening! And at evening you shall say, Oh, that it were morning! because of the fear which terrifies your heart, and because of the sight which your eyes see. [68] And YHWH will take you back to Mitsrayim in ships, by the way of which I said to you, You shall never see it again. And there you shall be offered for sale to your enemies as male and female slaves, but no one will buy you." Devarim 28:15-68.

I know this was a long passage but I hope that you took the time to read all of the curses associated with disobedience. The curses are extensive and specific which goes to show that this is serious business. Again, at this point, I can hear the standard retort of many Dispensationalists who will raise the objection that YHWH was speaking to Yisrael - not the Church. This, of course, is correct because there was no such thing as "the Church" and there was no such thing as Christianity

when these words were spoken.

The only "called out assembly" (qahal) that was present on Earth which was set apart to serve YHWH was Yisrael and any foreigners, strangers or sojourners that joined with them. At that point in time, these were the people that YHWH gave His commands. Today, if a person chooses to believe in Yahushua, the Hebrew Messiah, and follow the Elohim of Yisrael, he or she becomes adopted into the set apart assembly or "grafted in."

They become part of the Covenant which makes them eligible to receive the blessings as well as the curses. Take a look and examine the curses and see if they are not prevalent today. Now ask yourself if you would like these curses upon you and your family - maybe even now you are experiencing some of them. Once a person makes the decision to follow YHWH, they are subject to the blessings and curses which He promises to His people.

Now I know that YHWH is merciful and while many of His children are ignorant - they may not be experiencing the curses associated with their disobedience because it is not a willful and decided disobedience. I speak from experience because I blundered my way through His commandments most of my Christian existence and I know that He was merciful with me. Ultimately though, it is not His desire for His children to remain in ignorance – He wants us to repent and walk according to His Ways. (see Acts 17:30).

If you are reading this book and things are starting to become clear regarding the Torah, then He is being merciful to you also and it is time to repent. Eventually, all who have disobeyed will be punished whether or not

it was out of ignorance – the only difference will be the degree. (Luke 12:47-48).

14

Christianity and the Torah

While growing up in a mainstream Protestant denomination, nobody ever taught me how to live a life of obedience and I never really matured greatly in my spiritual walk. There comes a time when every child needs to grow up and it is time for Believers to grow up and move into the fullness of the promises and blessings of YHWH.

The following words are just as relevant today as when they were written to the early Assembly. "[12] *Though by this time you ought to be teachers, you need someone to teach you the elementary truths of Elohim's Word all over again. You need milk, not solid food!* [13] ***Anyone who lives on milk, being still an infant, is not acquainted with the teaching about righteousness.*** [14] *But solid food is for the mature, who by constant use have trained themselves to distinguish good from evil.*" Ibrim 5:12-6:1.

In other words, until you grow up you are not ready to learn about how to live righteously. This is consistent with the directives of the Yahrushalayim Council that we read about in Acts 15 and sadly, this is the current state of much of the Christian religion. Most Believers are still being fed milk. Week after week they hear the same

thematic sermons and they receive the same "altar" calls,[103] but rarely do they get solid food for righteous living so they can grow up.[104] Repeatedly, in the headlines, we read about Christian "leaders" who fall into sin and scandal because, having rejected or ignored the Torah, they lack a solid foundation and a standard for righteousness in their lives.

The Torah is all about righteous living and it is intended for a nation of Priests. ***Every human being is a creation of YHWH but only those who practice righteousness through obedience are called Children of Elohim.*** If you are a child of Elohim, then you have become a member of the Household of YHWH and you need to live by "the rules of the house." These rules are meant for our own good so that the Family of Elohim can live together in unity and in a way that is pleasing to YHWH. The rejection of Torah by mainstream Christianity is probably much of the reason for the division and disunity found within the Church. The family cannot agree and get along because they do not follow the rules.

Regarding Torah observance and our ability to obey all of the Torah, there is an aspect of common sense which must be recognized. If a commandment relates to a woman and you are a man, then you obviously do not need to obey it. I think that most people would find that much of the Torah is straightforward and easy to understand. With a little study and prayer, any Christian could start to become Torah observant in no time at all. I would suggest reviewing Acts 15 and do exactly what was directed - start with the necessities and go through the Torah cycle. Begin studying the Torah and walking in truth as it applies to your circumstances.

In response to this suggestion one might ask: What about the mitzvot relating to the Temple Service and the Priests? How can we possibly obey those mitzvot when the Temple has been destroyed and there is no functioning Levitic priesthood? This is a fair question and the answer is simpler than one might think and has been given to us in the Scriptures.

"[9] *But* ***you are*** *a chosen people,* ***a royal priesthood,*** *a holy nation, a people belonging to Elohim, that you may declare the praises of Him who called you out of darkness into His wonderful light.* [10] *Once you were not a people, but now you are the people of Elohim; once you had not received mercy, but now you have received mercy.*" 1 Kepha 2:9-10. Kepha was quoting the Prophet Hoshea and was speaking about the House of Yisrael - the 10 Northern Tribes - being regathered and restored – He is not talking about Levites.

In the Letter to the Ibrim we are told: "[24] *but because Yahushua lives forever, He has a permanent priesthood.* [25] *Therefore He is able to save completely those who come to Elohim through Him, because He always lives to intercede for them.* [26] *Such a high priest meets our need - one Who is holy, blameless, pure, set apart from sinners, exalted above the heavens.* [27] *Unlike the other high priests, He does not need to offer sacrifices day after day, first for His own sins, and then for the sins of the people. He sacrificed for their sins once for all when He offered Himself.*" Ibrim 7:24-27.

We read that we are all priests if Yahushua is our High Priest. "[5] *To Him who loves us and has freed us from our sins by his blood,* [6] *and has made us to be a kingdom and priests to serve his Elohim and Father - to Him be glory and power for ever and ever! Amen.*" Revelation 1:5-6.

We are also living tabernacles. "*Or do you not know*

that ***your body is the temple of the Holy Spirit who is in you,*** *whom you have from Elohim, and you are not your own?"* 1 Corinthians 6:19. "[16] *What agreement is there between the temple of Elohim and idols? For* ***we are the temple of the living Elohim.*** *As Elohim has said: I will live with them and walk among them, and I will be their Elohim, and they will be my people.* [17] *Therefore come out from them and be separate, says* YHWH. ***Touch no unclean thing, and I will receive you.*** [18] *I will be a Father to you, and you will be my sons and daughters, says* YHWH *Almighty."* 2 Corinthians 6:16-18.[105]

Our High Priest offered the ultimate sacrifice - that of atonement for our sins, as only a High Priest can do. We offer spiritual sacrifices instead of bulls and goats and we are being built into a living Temple. "[4] *As you come to Him, the living Stone - rejected by men but chosen by Elohim and precious to Him -* [5] *you also, like living stones, are being built into a spiritual house to be a holy priesthood, offering spiritual sacrifices acceptable to Elohim through Yahushua Messiah."* 1 Kepha 2:4-6. This does not mean that the physical Temple System has been abolished by any means. In fact, the Scriptures reveal that it will be reestablished.

At the same time, as the Living Temple and as Priests of the Most High, Believers are to be "qadosh" (קדש) which means to be set apart or holy unto YHWH. We are to be clean – both physically and spiritually and we are instructed not to touch any unclean thing or eat anything unclean[106] and our thoughts and intentions are to be pure as well.

So how are we supposed to know what is unclean and what is clean? The Torah, of course. Look at the example of Messiah and prayerfully consider the application of these instructions to your journey of faith. Use them to

help in your priestly service - your walk and relationship with YHWH will never be the same.

With this understanding we can blow the dust off of the Torah and see the present and future relevance of these Scriptures which many have taught were outdated and only for the "Jews." If you plan on living in the Kingdom of YHWH and serving as a priest, then I suggest you start studying the Torah so that you know how to live and serve in the Kingdom. I am not talking about some future event when you get whisked away into the clouds.[107] I am talking about here and now because once a person believes and repents, they become citizens in the Kingdom and their service starts immediately.

I liken it to a group of immigrants who get off a boat on Ellis Island - the historical immigrant processing center in America. They need to obtain their citizenship inorder to become official. Often times they need to go through certain procedures, take classes, study the language, learn the culture, get a job, take an oath to obey the law of the land - the constitution - and pledge allegiance to the flag - the banner which symbolizes the nation. They need to do all of these things so that they will be properly equipped to function within society.

As citizens of the Kingdom of YHWH we too must learn the law (Torah), the language (Hebrew) and serve in our capacity in the Kingdom. To be good citizens we should learn, obey and subject ourselves to our leader – Messiah. We do not just become citizens in a nation - we become members of a family. Therefore, it is more like

becoming a citizen of a Kingdom and at that very instant the King summons you and asks you to join the royal family. Not only does He adopt you, but he gives you all of the rights and privileges of a first born!

Now, with that in mind, imagine the enormity of the deception which has been perpetrated upon many Christians - a group of people who claim to be a Royal Priesthood and a Holy Nation. (1 Kepha 2:9). Instead they are, in large part, living defiled lives, unable to properly minister to YHWH, and having rejected the Torah of the Kingdom, finding themselves locked out of the Feast of the Universe because they are lawless. Of course, this is the desired goal of the Deceiver and the lawless one: "*to deceive even the elect.*"

Those who believe in Yahushua are called to live holy lives. The word holy is properly translated as "set apart." Holy or set apart living involves distinguishing between right and wrong, holy and unholy, clean and unclean. We learn all of these things from the Torah. Yahushua clearly taught this when He stated: "*Do not give what is set apart to the dogs, nor throw your pearls before the swines, lest they trample them under their feet, and turn and tear you to pieces.*" Mattithyahu 7:6.

Regrettably, Christians do not fully grasp this message because they do not regard swine as unclean. Since Yahushua, in His earthly ministry, was speaking to Yisrealites who were Torah observant He was invoking vivid images that the lawless Gentile mind may not pick up on. You see dogs and pigs are unclean according to the Torah - this is specifically why Yahushua often used those animals in His parables and ministry.

The ideal citizen of any nation should be legalistic,

in so far as those laws are just and true and do not contradict the Torah of YHWH. We all make legalistic pledges and take legalistic oaths as citizens of the nation to which we belong. We agree to adhere to the law of the land, thus we agree to be legalistic toward the laws of man. Why then is it considered wrong to be obedient toward the instructions and commandments of YHWH?

If we are truly citizens of the Kingdom of Heaven, a holy Nation and a royal priesthood (Shemoth 19:6; 1 Kepha 2:9) we must realize that we are subject to the rule of the Kingdom which is the Torah. The Torah is, in essence, the "Constitution" of the Kingdom of Heaven. The only caveat is to be legalistic as our King, High Priest and Rabbi Messiah Yahushua was legalistic – not like the religious men and women that He rebuked.

There is nothing wrong with legalism when it involves a person's diligent attempts to obey the Commandments of YHWH out of love. We must realize that we were born in sin, therefore even if you began this instant to obey the Torah perfectly, it would not and could not earn you salvation: "*For all have sinned and fall short of the Glory of YHWH.*"(Romans 3:23).

As a result, we are all blemished and YHWH does not accept a blemished sacrifice, it is an abomination to Him. (Devarim 17:1). Therefore our desire to obey is not rooted in an attempt to earn our salvation, but rather from our love and appreciation and our desire to please the One Who saved us from everlasting damnation. This is the sort of conduct and attitude which is pleasing to our Heavenly Father.

The religious leaders who sought to kill Yahushua demonstrated the type of legalism that leads to bondage

because they did not simply believe in obeying the instructions of YHWH. Instead, they took the Torah and added their own rules and regulations, and eventually replaced the Torah with their own customs and traditions, which was a direct violation of Torah. "*Whatever I command you, be careful to observe it;* ***you shall not add to it nor take away from it.***" (Devarim 4:2; 12:32).

They took the Perfect Law of Liberty (Ya'akov 1:25) which leads to freedom and righteousness and made it a burden too heavy for men to bear - they ended up turning men into slaves. This is what improper legalism does, instead of giving life - it leads to bondage and death. Yahushua always advocated obeying the Torah but chastised the religious leaders for adding to the Torah and for being hypocrites. Notice though, that adding is not the only sin - taking away is also a sin. Therefore, where the religious leaders in Yahushua's day sinned by adding to the Torah, the modern Christian "Church" sins by taking away from the Torah and by teaching that it was abolished or inapplicable.

In reality, every Christian is legalistic to some extent - they all have a set of things which they believe are right and things which they believe are wrong. Some will drink alcohol while others do not. This is a hot button issue despite the fact that there is no restriction in the Torah regarding drinking. In fact, there are portions which specifically encourage and permit strong drink and wine. (Devarim 14:26).

Of course, the Scriptures warn that it is unwise to drink to excess (Proverbs (Mishle) 20:1) and it is sinful to be a drunkard. (1 Corinthians 5:11). Notwithstanding, the drink offering was made to show us what it means

to feast with YHWH and it is definitely <u>not</u> a sin to consume alcoholic beverages. If you believe this then you are thumbing your nose at something which has been condoned and even sanctified by the Almighty.

There are some who do not believe in dancing, while a plain reading of Scripture shows that dancing is a form of worship unto YHWH. King Dawid leapt and danced to YHWH. (2 Shemuel 6:16). Some do not believe in using instruments during worship despite the fact that the use of instruments during praise and worship is mentioned throughout the Scriptures. (Tehillim 150).

Some believe that smoking is sinful although there is no mention of smoking in the Scriptures. I could go on and on but I think that I made my point.

Every individual has their own list of conduct which they deem to be appropriate and which they deem to be inappropriate. The only question that matters is whether their list lines up with the Torah. It does not matter what <u>I think</u> is right or wrong. It only matters what <u>YHWH says</u> is right or wrong and He does not have to explain Himself.

What I find so remarkable is the hypocrisy that I so often observe, and once lived, in Christianity. Some Christians will call a person legalistic who endeavors to observe the Torah while they themselves live a life of lawlessness. They will then turn around and try to impose their legalistic beliefs on others – beliefs which are not supported by the Torah. What they fail to realize is that they are the ones who are legalistic. This type of hypocrisy is what Shaul was referring to when he proclaimed:

"*Indeed, all matters are clean to the clean, but to those who are defiled and unbelieving no matter is clean, but both their mind and conscience are defiled. They profess to know Elohim, but in works they deny Him, being abominable, and disobedient, and unfit for any good work.*" Titus 1:15-16.

I will never forget an incident in college ministry when I was trying to use a Christian tract to explain to my atheist roommate the difference between the fruits of righteousness and the fruits of sin. This tract contained a picture of two trees – the tree of righteousness and the tree of sin. On each tree were fruits - the tree of righteousness had those fruits listed by Shaul in Galatians 5:22 – love, joy, peace, longsuffering, kindness, goodness, faithfulness, gentleness and self control. On the other tree were things such as tobacco, alcohol, dancing and swearing along with some of the works of the flesh listed by Shaul in Galatians 5:19. My atheist roommate proceeded to ask me where in the Bible it said a person could not dance, smoke or drink alcohol. I had to admit that it did not.

The Christians who wrote the tract were no doubt well meaning and clearly were envisioning someone hanging out in a bar, drinking until they are intoxicated, smoking and dancing in revelry and then going and committing fornication. Sadly though, the tract portrayed a legalism which was not Scriptural and my atheist roommate won that round. This is why it is important that we obey the Torah and not start adding our own man-made rules and regulations – that is when we start getting into trouble and clouding the Truth.

As previously stated, most Christians will admit that they must obey the Ten Commandments. In fact, there have been many legal battles by Christian groups

to keep the Ten Commandments in schools and in the courts. I find it ironic how hard they will fight to display the commandments and how quickly they will dismiss the 4th Commandment concerning the Sabbath.

When asked about the 4th Commandment Christians will quickly say that this commandment does not apply to them, that "Jesus changed the Sabbath for Christians" or "Jesus is Lord of the Sabbath" or "every day is the Sabbath." None of these answers provide a justification for changing the Sabbath Day to Sunday. A failure to understand the Sabbath is a failure to understand the Creator and it is critical that every Christian take a fresh look at this issue and throw out all of the false doctrine which has been instilled in them throughout their lives.[108]

It is equally interesting how Christian groups will attempt to assert their moral agenda on society when the basis for their belief is only found in the Torah. Issues such as abortion, homosexuality and same sex marriage can only properly be confronted with the Torah of YHWH. Christians who promote the morality found in the Torah while advocating the abolition or irrelevance of the Torah are quite simply hypocrites and will not find much traction for their arguments.

The problem with the Christian approach to the Ten Commandments is the same problem with the Christian approach to the Letter to the Gentile converts from the Yahrushalayim Council. Christianity is continually trying to separate and distinguish itself from what they perceive as "Jewish." Instead of just obeying the Torah, they often try to find reasons why they should

not or do not have to obey the Torah of YHWH.

Think about how our Heavenly Father must view this attitude. As a parent, it can get pretty discouraging when your child will not obey your clear directives, yet it is so satisfying when your child not only does what you tell them, but obeys without having to be told and does so willingly and joyfully. YHWH gives us these real life relationships and examples so that we can understand what He expects from His children. His hope for us is that we obey Him - not just because we have to - His longing is that we obey because we want to. The heart of the Torah is that we obey - not for the rewards - but out of love.

Too often, instead of obedience, Christians profess that they do not have to obey because they are "under grace." If that is what you believe then I suppose children do not have to obey parents any longer. Can you imagine a child pronouncing to a parent that they did not have to obey the rules of the house because they are under grace and not under law. I doubt that such an argument would find much success. Likewise I doubt a judge or police officer would agree that it is alright for you to speed because you are under grace. Why should the instructions of the Creator be treated any different?

Our heart determines how we perceive the Torah - whether we view it as instructions that aid us or as law that enslaves us. The obedient son is the one who gladly receives "instruction" from his father. He understands that it is for his own good so he endeavors to learn, obey and prosper from the instruction. The disobedient son receives the "law" of his father and sees it as a burden - something that he must obey. He typically spends his time trying to find ways not to obey and this heart attitude

often leads to rebellion.

The instructions to each son are the same but the heart determines how they are perceived. The obedient son sees the instructions as life giving and desires to obey while the disobedient son sees the instructions as law and bondage. He does not desire to obey and either rebels completely or obeys as little as possible. Each of us must determine which category we fall within – if in fact we fall within one of them at all. Some reject the instruction altogether and find themselves living in a state of lawlessness.

15

Lawlessness

The misapplication of grace within Christianity and the lack of a healthy fear of YHWH has led to a near wholesale rejection of the Torah by the Christian community. This begs the question: If Yahushua stated that not one yud or stroke would pass away until all is fulfilled then how did Christianity get to the present state of selective obedience - or should I say disobedience - because there is no room to be on the fence with this issue. You cannot pick and choose which commandments that you want to obey. You either choose to be obedient or you choose to be disobedient. To be disobedient is to be in a state of lawlessness.

If we fail to obey the Torah, we are in sin. Yahanan clearly reveals this truth by stating: "***Everyone who sins breaks the Torah; in fact, sin is lawlessness.***" 1 Yahanan 3:4. You will not find this statement in most modern English translations of the text but this is a literal translation from the Greek. The writings of Shaul make a clear distinction between righteousness and lawlessness. "*For what fellowship has righteousness with lawlessness? And what communion has light with darkness?*" 2 Corinthians 6:15 NKJV. We can see from this passage of Scripture that righteousness is the

opposite of lawlessness. Righteousness involves obedience and lawlessness involves disobedience - it is that simple.

Now let us examine what the Messiah Himself has to say about lawlessness. "[21] *Not everyone who says to Me, 'Lord, Lord,' shall enter the kingdom of heaven, but he who does the will of My Father in heaven.*[22] *Many will say to Me in that day, 'Lord, Lord, have we not prophesied in Your Name, cast out demons in Your Name, and done many wonders in Your Name?'*[23] *And then I will declare to them, '<u>I never knew you; depart from Me, you who practice lawlessness!</u>'*" Mattithyahu 7:21-23 NKJV.

Some translations use the word "iniquity" instead of "lawlessness." The Greek word for both iniquity and lawlessness in this passage is "anomia" (ανομὶα) which refers to a transgressor of the Torah: someone who is wicked and unrighteous. Therefore, this passage may be translated "***Depart from Me you who disobey the Torah.***"

J. P. Green, Sr. in his Interlinear New Testament references Tehillim 6:8 when translating this passage. In Tehillim, King Dawid cries out: "*Depart from me, all who work iniquity, for YHWH has heard the voice of my weeping.*" The Hebrew word for iniquity in the Tehillim is "aven" (און) and also means wicked and unrighteousness.

With the understanding that lawlessness is a state of living in disobedience to the Torah - let us take a moment to see if we can figure out the identity of this group of people referred to by Yahushua. It would seem reasonable that no one in their right mind would want to be found in this group. These people appear to be doing things which, on the surface would be considered powerful, anointed and proper - yet they are lawless and therefore they are rejected by the Messiah.

First of all there are a lot of them because the Scripture refers to "*many*" in this group. Second, they call the Messiah "Lord" or "Master" which would lead one to believe that they are familiar with the Messiah and acknowledge His Kingship. The fact that the Scriptures repeat "*Lord, Lord*" is a way of providing emphasis on this word. These people are emphatic in their calling upon the Messiah as "Lord" – they are likely crying out with loud and desparate shouts. Third, they are prophesying, casting out demons and doing mighty works "allegedly" in His Name. Fourth, they are lawless - in other words - they are living in disobedience to the Torah.

Finally, Yahushua stated that He never knew them - despite the fact they seem to think that they not only know Him but have been serving Him. I feel that is directly related to the fact that His Name is Yahushua while most Christians insist upon calling Him Jesus - a name with pagan origins. It appears that this group is calling upon a name and doing mighty works in a name which they believe is the Messiah's, but they are incorrect and therefore do not really know the true Messiah.

Besides not knowing His Name, their conduct also has a direct effect on their relationship. The Scriptures clearly set forth the connection between continuing in sin and knowing the Messiah. "[5] *But you know that He appeared so that He might take away our sins. And in Him is no sin.* [6] ***No one who lives in Him keeps on sinning. No one who continues to sin has either seen Him or known Him.***" 1 Yahanan 3:5-6 NIV. Therefore, if you think that you know the Messiah and continue to disobey His Torah then you are deceived because lawlessness is sin. You do not really know Him and possibly never knew Him.

So who is this large group of lawless people who think that they know the Hebrew Messiah and who are prophesying, casting out demons and doing mighty works, "allegedly" in His Name? As far as I can see the only group on the face of the earth that fits this particular description is the Christian Church.

This actually makes perfect sense because the messiah that the Christian Church presents to the world does not line up with the true Hebrew Messiah. So depending upon where a person was introduced to the Messiah, they may have never met Yahushua HaMashiach - they may have been introduced to an imposter, a false messiah. To put it another way, they may have met the anti-Messiah, the lawless one who through the secret power of lawlessness is attempting to take the place of the true Messiah of Yisrael, who will deceive the very elect, if possible.

In the Good News according to Luke, the Messiah gives us another look at this same scenario involving a group of lawless people. "[24] *Strive to enter through the narrow gate, for many, I say to you, will seek to enter and will not be able.*[25] *When once the Master of the house has risen up and shut the door, and you begin to stand outside and knock at the door, saying, Lord, Lord, open for us, and He will answer and say to you, I do not know you, where you are from,* [26] *then you will begin to say, we ate and drank in Your presence, and You taught in our streets.* [27] *But He will say, I tell you I do not know you, where you are from.* ***Depart from Me, all you workers of iniquity***. [28] *There will be weeping and gnashing of teeth, when you see Avraham and Yitshaq and Ya'akov and all the prophets in the Kingdom of Elohim, and yourselves thrust out.*[29] *They will come from the east and the west, from the north and the south,*

and sit down in the Kingdom of Elohim. [30] And indeed there are last who will be first, and there are first who will be last." Luke 13:24-30.

The Greek word for iniquity in this passage is "adikos" (αδικία) which also means *wickedness and unrighteousness.* Interestingly, J. P. Green, Sr. again references Psalm 6:8 when translating this passage. While two different words are used to describe this group of people in the Greek manuscripts, they appear to be one and the same according to the Messiah. They are workers of iniquity - *wicked, unrighteous and lawless.* Strong's Complete Dictionary of Bible Words goes so far as to define lawless in this context as not being subject to the "Jewish Law," which is, of course, referring to the Torah.

This is a very important and powerful message coming straight from the Messiah and it does not seem that it could be presented any clearer. In both instances He states that He does not know the people who are calling to Him and in both instances it is clear that He does not know them because of their state of lawlessness.

This point is reinforced further in the Messianic Scriptures as follows: "[3] ***Now by this we know that we know Him, if we keep His commandments.*** [4] ***He who says, I know Him, and does not keep His commandments, is a liar, and the truth is not in him.*** [5] *But whoever keeps His word, truly the love of Elohim is perfected in him. By this we know that we are in Him.* [6] *He who says he abides in Him ought himself also to walk just as He walked.* [7] ***Brethren, I write no new commandment to you, but an old commandment which you have had from the beginning. The old commandment is the word which you heard from the beginning.***" 1 Yahanan 2:3-7.

Yahanan reaffirms that knowledge comes from

obedience to the commandments and that is how a person can be assured if they know the True Messiah: If they obey His commandments. Notice that he is clear that when he speaks of obedience he is not referring to any obscure new commandments but "*an old commandment which you have had from the beginning. The old commandment is the word which you heard from the beginning.*" Of course this is the same Yahanan that wrote the beautiful words: "*In the beginning was the Word, and the Word was with Elohim, and the Word was Elohim.*" Yahanan 1:1. It was the Messiah Who was and is the Word and therefore to obey Him is to obey the Torah. We are to walk as He walked - according to the Torah.

Why then is there so much confusion, unbelief and disobedience in Christianity related to the Torah? This is what Shaul meant when he spoke of the mystery of iniquity or, to put it another way, the mystery of lawlessness.

"[1] *Concerning the coming of our Master Yahushua the Messiah and our being gathered to Him, we ask you, brothers,* [2] *not to become easily unsettled or alarmed by some prophecy, report or letter supposed to have come from us, saying that the day of YHWH has already come.* [3] *Do not let anyone deceive you in any way, for that day will not come until the rebellion occurs and* <u>*the man of lawlessness is revealed*</u>*, the man doomed to destruction.* [4] *He will oppose and will exalt himself over everything that is called Elohim or is worshiped, so that he sets himself up in the Temple of Elohim, proclaiming himself to be Elohim.* [5] *Don't you remember that when I was with you I used to tell you these things?* [6] *And now you know what is holding him back, so that he may be revealed at the proper time.* [7] ***For the secret power of lawlessness is already at work;*** *but the one who now holds it back will continue to do so till he is taken out of*

the way. [8] *And then the lawless one will be revealed, whom the Master will overthrow with the breath of his mouth and destroy by the splendor of his coming.* [9] *The coming of the lawless one will be in accordance with the work of Satan displayed in all kinds of counterfeit miracles, signs and wonders,* [10] *and in every sort of evil that deceives those who are perishing.* ***They perish because they refused to love the truth and so be saved.*** [11] ***For this reason Elohim sends them a powerful delusion so that they will believe the lie*** [12] ***and so that all will be condemned who have not believed the truth but have delighted in wickedness.***" 2 Thessalonians 2:1-12.

Anyone even slightly familiar with the prophecies in Daniel and Revelation would recognize this lawless one to be the anti-christ also known as the anti-messiah. People often get the wrong impression of who the lawless one will be because the use of "anti" is a bit misleading. "Anti" in the Greek is a primary particle which means not only, "opposite or in opposition" which is the common understanding, but also "instead of or in substitution."

So not only does the anti-messiah oppose the true Messiah, but he also wants to replace the Messiah and substitute himself for the Messiah and be worshiped like Elohim. Therefore where Messiah obeyed the Torah, supported the Torah and taught the Torah (thus the title Rabbi - Teacher), the lawless one, or anti-messiah, promotes disobedience to the Torah through "*the secret power of lawlessness.*"

He does not want people to obey, because obedience leads to relationship, knowledge and blessing. He does not want people to know YHWH nor does he want them to be blessed. "*He shall speak pompous words against the Most High, shall persecute the saints of the Most High,* ***and shall***

intend to change times and law. *Then the saints shall be given into his hand for a time and times and half a time."* Daniel 7:25 NKJV.

Notice from the passage in Thessalonians Shaul stated that the secret power of lawlessness was already at work. A review of the history of early believers shows that anti-nomianism - against the Torah - was very prevalent. This is something which the early Apostles spent much time combating. This was due in large part to the massive influx of pagan Gentiles who flooded the early assembly of Believers - often times bringing some of their pagan practices and beliefs with them. (see Acts 8:9-24).

We have a great promise with regard to knowing YHWH and it is found in the Renewed Covenant: "[33] *This is the Covenant I will make with the House of Yisrael after that time, declares YHWH. I will put my Torah in their minds and write it on their hearts. I will be their Elohim, and they will be my people.* [34] *No longer will a man teach his neighbor, or a man his brother, saying, Know YHWH, because they will all know Me, from the least of them to the greatest, declares YHWH. For I will forgive their wickedness and will remember their sins no more."* Yirmeyah 31:33-34.

There will soon come a day when YHWH will introduce Himself in such a way that there will be no mistaking who He is, but until that time the spirit of lawlessness is working feverishly to lead men toward disobedience and lawlessness - away from knowing the true Elohim. While the Messiah Yahushua taught and lived the Torah – Christianity worships and promotes Jesus, who allegedly changed or abolished the Torah. He has been promoted as a lawless messiah and I trust that the problem is now apparent.

I for one believe that we are in the last days so it makes perfect sense that the secret power of lawlessness is here, deluding people in preparation for the appearance of anti-messiah. Many might ask, how could this happen to Believers? We have been warned by the Messiah Himself. "[11] *Then many false prophets will rise up and deceive many.*[12] *And because **lawlessness will abound**, the love of many will grow cold*." Mattityahu 24:11-12. "[24] *For false messiahs and false prophets will rise and show great signs and wonders to deceive, if possible, even the elect.*[25] *See, I have told you beforehand.*" Mattithyahu 24:24-25.

To this day, untaught and unstable teachers are using the writings of Shaul to twist the Scriptures and undermine the Torah. It is important to read on and see where this leads. "*You, then, beloved ones, being forewarned, watch, lest you also fall from your own steadfastness, being led away with the delusion of lawlessness*." 2 Kepha 3:17.

The delusion of lawlessness is the false teaching that you do not have to obey the Torah. This is the same delusion referred to by Shaul in his letter to the Thessalonians (2 Thessalonians 2:1-12), the same lawlessness referred to by Yahanan. (1 Yahanan 3:4) and it is the same error referred to by Yahushua. (Mattityahu 7:23; Luke 13:24-30).

For those who profess to "know Elohim" but practice lawlessness it is time to rethink your concept of the Torah and grace. Kepha taught both grace and obedience: "[13] *Therefore gird up the loins of your mind, be sober, and **rest your hope fully upon the grace that is to be brought to you at the revelation** of Yahushua Hamashiach;* [14] ***as obedient children**, not conforming yourselves to the former lusts, as in your ignorance;*[15] *but as He who called you is holy, you also be holy in all your conduct,*[16] *because it is written, 'Be holy, for I am*

holy.'" 1 Kepha 1:13-16.

As Kepha aptly demonstrated, the Torah and grace are not in opposition to one another, but rather allies in the Eternal plan of YHWH. A good way to illustrate this point is to describe the Torah as a container and the Messiah as the living water which is poured into the container. You need the container to receive the water. Without the container, the water spills on the ground and we are unable to drink.

This partnership between the Torah and grace is aptly demonstrated by the traditional belief that the Torah was given to the Children of Yisrael on Shavuot (Pentecost) and the Spirit was also given to the talmidim of Messiah on Shavuot (Pentecost).[109] The Torah given on the same day as the Spirit - this is no coincidence. The Spirit writes the Torah on our hearts and in our minds and empowers us to live the Torah just as Messiah was the Living Torah.

16

The Walk of Faith

It is my hope that with the foundation provided by the Words of YHWH it is now evident that all Believers should be obeying the Torah. Once we understand the operation of grace and Torah and once we have received the gift of forgiveness, it is important that we then start to walk with our Creator. As the Creator walked with Adam and Yisrael and as the Messiah walked with His talmidim - so too - He wants to walk with us. Our life is our walk, it is the training ground to learn His ways.

This walk that I am referring to is often called halakah (הלכה) in Hebrew. It is the walk of faith which every Believer must walk. The tradition associated with Judaism has often made halakah a burden by requiring adherents to follow their "oral Torah" but in the purest sense - it is the journey of faith that each of us, as individuals, must make with our Creator.

Thankfully, we do not have to walk in darkness - for we have been given Light. His Word is a lamp to our feet and it lights the path before us. (Tehillim 119:105). While the commentaries of teachers may be helpful, at times, it is our own individual responsibility to study, pray and walk perfectly before YHWH. His Torah reveals the

obstacles which lie before us and it shows us how to avoid them. The Torah is the straight path and it is the Way that all of the Children of YHWH must walk.

"*And you shall enlighten them concerning the laws and the Torot, and* ***show them the way in which they should walk*** *and the work which they do.*" Shemoth 18:20 The Scriptures. "[6] *And these Words which I am commanding you today shall be in your heart,* [7] *and you shall impress them upon your children, and you shall speak them when you sit in your house, and* ***when you walk by the way,*** *and when you lie down, and when you rise up.*" Devarim 6:7.

There are blessings when we walk in the way of the Torah. "[1] *Blessed is the man who walks not in the counsel of the ungodly, nor stands in the path of sinners, nor sits in the seat of the scornful;* [2] *But his delight is in the Torah of YHWH, and in His Torah he meditates day and night.*" Tehillim 1:1-2.

The reason why it is called a walk is because it often requires movement. This walk of faith takes much more than belief - it takes action. From the very definition of Torah in Chapter 2 we saw that it points the way and also requires movement in the direction which it points. Many in the Christian religion were introduced to the Messiah through a simple prayer where they acknowledged that they were a sinner and that they needed a Savior. While they may have verbalized their belief – it is not enough if they do not walk out that belief.

This is what Ya'akov meant when he said: "[17] *faith by itself, if it does not have works, is dead.* [18] *But someone will say, You have faith, and I have works. Show me your faith without your works, and I will show you my faith by my works.* [19] *You believe that there is one Elohim. You do well. Even the demons believe - and tremble!* [20] *But do you want to know, O foolish*

man, that faith without works is dead? [21] *Was not Avraham our father justified by works when he offered Yitshaq his son on the altar?* [22] *Do you see that faith was working together with his works, and by works faith was made perfect?*" Ya'akov 2:17-22.

This point vividly demonstrates the difference between Eastern and Western thought. Hebrew, being an Eastern Semitic language, is an active language while Greek is a Western language which tends to be passive. A person's language controls their perception and understanding of words and concepts and "faith" is a good example of this difference.

Faith and belief in Hebrew require action. In other words in Eastern thought you should have a corresponding outward act as a demonstration of your inward belief. In Western thought we have developed a mentality that the inward "decision" is what is important. A person can go to a revival meeting or crusade, make a "decision" and say a prayer, and they are often taught that that inward "decision" gives them an irrevocable ticket to heaven no matter how they live their lives.

Doctrines such as Eternal Security which teach "once saved, always saved" are potentially dangerous because as Ya'akov said – "*even demons believe.*" Believing in Elohim or acknowledging that He exists is quite meaningless, in and of itself - He exists whether or not you <u>decide</u> to believe it. It is whether we walk with Him that matters. If you truly have faith you will <u>both believe</u> what He says <u>and do</u> what He says – then your faith will be made perfect.

To walk according to the Torah is to walk the righteous path. The Torah teaches distinctions between

holy and profane, clean and unclean. It outlines the conduct required to live in the Kingdom and likewise it identifies those who are in the Kingdom by their actions. Those who live within the boundaries of the Torah are in the Kingdom - they are set apart from those outside the Kingdom.

It could not be any clearer from the following passage: "[3] *Now by this we know that we know Him, if we keep His commandments.* [4] *He who says, I know Him, and does not keep His commandments, is a liar, and the truth is not in him.* [5] *But whoever keeps His word, truly the love of Elohim is perfected in him. By this we know that we are in Him.* [6] *He who says he abides in Him* ***ought himself also to walk just as He walked***." 1 Yahanan 2:3-6. It means set yourself apart and walk in the ways that Messiah - the Torah in flesh walked.

Now again I want to reiterate so there is no mistake where I am coming from - we obey, not to obtain salvation - salvation is a free gift and cannot be earned. We obey - not to obtain blessings - that is a residual effect of our obedience. Rather we obey because we have voluntarily become bond servants of the Messiah. "*I speak in human terms because of the weakness of your flesh. For just as you presented your members as slaves of uncleanness, and of lawlessness leading to more lawlessness,* ***so now present your members as slaves of righteousness for holiness.***" Romans 6:19 NKJV.

Those who follow Messiah have agreed to become His talmidim and as such - obedience is expected. If you choose not to obey His commandments then you cannot call yourself His talmidim - regardless of whether or not you are doing what you think is right and good. The object

is to do what He tells us to do - not what we decide we should do. If you are not obeying His commandments then you are walking in disobedience and you can expect to hear the words – "*Depart from Me you who practice lawlessness.*"

"[7] *Therefore, to you who believe, He is precious; but to those who are disobedient, The Stone which the builders rejected Has become the Chief Capstone,* [8] *and a Stone of stumbling and a Rock of offense.' They stumble, being disobedient to the Word, to which they also were appointed*." 1 Kepha 2:7-8. Notice Kepha pits those "*who believe*" against "*those who are disobedient.*" By doing so he makes disobedience equal to disbelief. If you want to stir up your faith, then start living like you believe your Elohim by obeying His commandments.

The bottom line is that the Christian religion proclaims that you should "love God" but not necessarily obey Him. They may go so far as to agree that we must obey Him, but they are usually unclear what they must obey and strangely enough they usually all agree that it is definitely ***not the Torah***. It must be something else, usually some rule, regulation, custom or tradition created by man.

To disobey the Torah is sin and to do so is inconsistent with everything taught in the Scriptures. It is absurd to think that YHWH spent thousands of years teaching His Torah to individuals and the Nations through Yisrael only to throw it all away and replace it with something different called grace - which has not been defined. If this is what you have been taught then you need to reexamine your understanding of the Scriptures.

All Catholics and Christians would do well to heed the words of Shaul: "[1] *What shall we say then? Shall we continue in sin that grace may abound?* [2] *Certainly not! How*

shall we who died to sin live any longer in it?" Romans 6:1-2 NKJV. He is telling us that we should not continue to sin because of grace and if we are not to continue to sin then that must mean we are to live according to the instructions of YHWH found within the Torah.

Dispensationalists put Avraham and Christians in different dispensations which then requires different methods of salvation. Their doctrine is confusing and erroneous - the faith that saved Avraham is the same faith that provides salvation to this day - faith in the promises of YHWH. When Avram was ninety years old YHWH appeared to Him. YHWH confirmed His Covenant with Avram and changed his name to Avraham. During that encounter He declared: "*I am El Shaddai* – ***walk before me and be perfect***." Beresheet 17:1.

This is the same command that Yahushua gave to His followers: "*Therefore, be perfect, as your Father in the heavens is perfect.*" Mattityahu 5:48. This is the same admonition given by Dawid which reveals what it means to be perfect. "*Blessed are the perfect in the way, who walk in the Torah of YHWH.*" Tehillim 119:1.

Just as Avraham was instructed to walk perfect, so we are instructed to walk perfect. We have obviously all sinned in the past, but it is the point in our lives where we receive and exercise the faith that has been given to us that a change is supposed to occur. Once we know YHWH, we are to walk perfect according to His Torah.

The Prophet Yirmeyahu declared: "*Thus saith* YHWH, *Stand in the ways and see, and ask for the old paths, where the good way is, and walk in it; and find rest for yourselves.*" Yirmeyahu 6:16. There is rest in the righteous way and there is life. "*In the way of righteousness is life, and*

in its pathway there is no death." Mishle 12:28.

When Yahushua declared to His talmidim "*follow Me*" He was inviting them on the path of life. Just as He invited them, so too He invites us and proclaims: "[29] *Take My yoke upon you and learn from Me, for I am gentle and lowly in heart, and you will find rest for your souls.* [30] *For My yoke is easy and My burden is light.*" Mattityahu 11:29-30. He is the Living Torah and in Him we find true rest and life, but in order to see these promises manifest in our lives - we must walk.

17

In the End

The final words of the Tanak in most Christian Bibles are from the Prophet Malachi who, speaking of the last days, makes it very clear how YHWH will deal with those who do not obey His Torah.

"1 *Surely the day is coming; it will burn like a furnace. All the arrogant and every evildoer will be stubble, and that day that is coming will set them on fire, says YHWH Almighty. Not a root or a branch will be left to them.* 2 *But for you who revere My Name, the Sun of Righteousness will rise with healing in its wings. And you will go out and leap like calves released from the stall.* 3 *Then you will trample down the wicked; they will be ashes under the soles of your feet on the day when I do these things, says YHWH Almighty.* 4 *Remember the Torah of my servant Mosheh, the decrees and laws I gave him at Horeb for all Yisrael.* 5 *See, I will send you the prophet Eliyahu before that great and dreadful day of YHWH comes.* 6 *He will turn the hearts of the fathers to their children, and the hearts of the children to their fathers; or else I will come and strike the land with a curse.*" Malachi 4:1-6.

The Prophet Malachi is referring to a time in the future and you will notice that we are instructed to *remember the Torah.* Recognize that the evildoers and

wicked are those who do not obey the Torah – they will be turned into stubble and ashes and trampled under foot.

I find it particularly interesting that this passage occurs immediately before the Messianic Scriptures in most Bibles because in the Hebrew Tanak the order is not the same – the Prophets come after the Torah and the writings come last. It is as if it was intentionally done as a reminder to Christians – right before we read about the Messiah because if read properly - there is nothing in the Messianic Scriptures which alters or conflicts with the Torah.

For instance, there is nothing which would change the commandment to circumcise your son on the eighth day, to rest on the Sabbath or any other instruction which relates to your particular circumstances. Yahushua did not come to abolish the Torah - He came to get people back to the purity of the Torah. Yahushua never had a problem with the Pharisees obeying the Torah. His concern was because they had substituted their own rules and regulations for the Torah of YHWH which resulted in them not keeping the Torah as prescribed by YHWH. Stephen confirmed this in his famous sermon in the Book of Acts. (Acts 7:53).

The Pharisees lost touch with the intent of the Torah which is meant to direct us to the Father and change us - Yahushua always directed people to the Father. This is what the Word (Torah) has always done. If Yahushua came to teach people to disobey the Word then He would have been a walking contradiction, The Torah in the flesh teaching people not to obey the Torah? It simply does not make any sense.

If you are not walking in obedience to the Torah

then you are walking in disobedience and you are one of the sons of disobedience rather than a son of Elohim. "[6] *Let no one deceive you with empty words, for because of these things the wrath of Elohim comes upon* ***the sons of disobedience.***[7] *Therefore do not be partakers with them.* [8] *For you were once darkness, but now you are light in YHWH. Walk as children of light* [9] *(for the fruit of the Spirit is in all goodness, righteousness, and truth),* [10] *finding out what is acceptable to YHWH."* Ephesians 5:5-10.

The sons of disobedience walk in darkness and are lawless while the children of light seek out what is acceptable to YHWH through His Torah and they walk in obedience - in the light of the Torah. This point is made very clear by the Prophet Yeshayahu: "*To the Torah and to the testimony (witness)! If they do not speak according to this Word, it is because there is no light in them.*" Yeshayahu 8:20.

The relationship between Torah and grace is not difficult to understand and reconcile once you have placed each in its proper place. It is the result of men manipulating the terms and ideas that they represent which has caused such confusion and placed them seemingly at odds with one another.

To say that the Torah was abolished effectively says that there is no longer any sin, since sin is defined by the Torah. Without the Torah we have no reference for sin which leads to anarchy, improper legalism and lawlessness. To believe and profess such a notion is nothing short of sin and leads to some very dangerous conclusions.

If you have been taught that the Torah is something to be avoided at all costs then you have been misled. If

you have been taught that YHWH gave His Torah to Yisrael but He exempted "The Church" from obeying the Torah, then once again - you have been misled. There is no commandment in the Messianic Scriptures instructing Gentile converts not to obey the Torah. If there were one it would not be correct because the only way to test a prophet or the teachings of a talmidim was through the Tanak. Just as the Bereans searched the Scriptures (Tanak) daily to verify the truth of Shaul's teachings - we should do the same. (Acts 17:11).

The Messianic Scriptures cannot alter the Tanak in any way because it is the Tanak which validates and supports those Scriptures. Christians have had centuries of programming to the contrary so this is often a difficult truth to grasp, but if you can renew your mind you will see your relationship with YHWH flower because all of the pieces to the puzzle will start falling into place. I spent much of my life in Christianity trying to force a square peg into a round hole and it never fit because their doctrine is inconsistent with the Tanak.

If you are a Christian and are relying on the promise of the Renewed Covenant then you had better heed the words of the Prophet Yehezqel. "[19] ***Then I will give them one heart, and I will put a new spirit within them, and take the stony heart out of their flesh, and give them a heart of flesh,*** [20] ***that they may walk in My statutes and keep My judgments and do them; and they shall be My people, and I will be their Elohim.***[21] ***But as for those whose hearts follow the desire for their detestable things and their abominations, I will recompense their deeds on their own heads,*** *says YHWH Elohim.*" Yehezqel 11:19-21.

In this passage the Prophet was speaking to the House of Yisrael, those who have been scattered, those

who have not obeyed the commandments and who have followed the ways of the Gentiles (Yehezqel 11:12). He reveals that the purpose of the Renewed Covenant is so: "***that they may walk in My statutes and keep My judgments and do them.***" This is an integral portion of the Renewed Covenant which Christianity fails to teach.

The passage further speaks of those who continue in lawlessness and for them the future is not very bright. Since we know that the Renewed Covenant is made with the House of Yisrael and the House of Yahudah - you need to first determine if you belong to the Commonwealth of Yisrael or to some other religion or organization which advocates a different covenant. Depending on your response you must then ask whether you are walking and keeping the statutes and judgments of YHWH. If not, then you are not a partaker of the Renewed Covenant and you are not walking in the Light.

The Messianic Scriptures speak of a spiritual war that has raged through the ages and will culminate with a great conflict described in the Revelation according to Yahanan. That conflict will revolve around a certain group of people specifically described. "*Then the dragon was enraged at the woman and went off to make war against the rest of her offspring - those who obey Elohim's commandments and hold to the testimony of Yahushua.*" Revelation 12:16-17. The set apart ones who endure to the end are repeatedly described as the ones who obey the commandments and remain faithful to Yahushua. (Revelation 14:12).

We have been given power to obey, to live righteously and to overcome sin through the blood of the Lamb and the Spirit (Ruach). When we receive the gift of the Ruach we are renewed beings with the Torah written

on our hearts and in our minds. "[4] *For whatever is born of Elohim overcomes the world. And this is the victory that has overcome the world - our faith.* [5] *Who is he who overcomes the world, but he who believes that Yahushua is the Son of Elohim*" 1 Yahanan 5:4-5.

By now the following Scripture should be clear: "*For while the Torah was given through Mosheh, grace and truth came through Yahushua the Messiah.*" Yahanan 1:17. While grace gives us the opportunity to have life, the truth of the Torah shows us how to live that life. This is the essence of the work of the Messiah - both grace and Torah are spiritual and they both lead to life. The grace of YHWH puts us on the path of life and the Torah is the path which leads to life.

Just as in the beginning man and woman had access to the Tree of Life until they disobeyed the commandment of YHWH, so in the end Redeemed mankind - those who obey the commandments - will once again have access to the Tree of Life.

"*Blessed are those <u>who do His commandments,</u> that they may have the right to the Tree of Life, and may enter through the gates into the city.*" Revelation 22:14. This is the promise in store for those who properly understand **"The Law"** and grace.

Endnotes

1 Yahushua - The correct Hebrew Name for the Messiah commonly called Jesus, is Yahushua (יהושע). It is the same Name as the Hebrew Patriarch commonly called Joshua and it means "Yah is salvation." Jesus is not the Name of the Messiah and it is a literal impossibility for Him to be called Jesus since there is no "J" sound in either the Hebrew or Greek languages. While many claim that the word "Jesus" is simply the English translation for the Hebrew Yahushua this is not accurate nor would it even be appropriate to use a translation while referring to the Name of the Messiah. You do not translate Names – you transliterate Names. Thus the English Yahushua is a transliteration of the Hebrew יהושע so that we know how to properly pronounce the Name. This subject is discussed in detail in The Walk in the Light Series book entitled "Names."

2 Messiah - I refer to Yahushua using a form of the Hebrew word moshiach (משיח) which is translated Messiah and means "anointed." When you refer to Yahushua as The Messiah, there is no question what you mean, especially in the context of the Hebrew Scriptures. The word "christ" is a Greek term which also means "anointed" but is applied to any number of their pagan gods. Therefore, the title Messiah seems more appropriate when referring to the Hebrew Moshiach.

3 The name of the Disciple commonly known as John in the English was a Hebrew and therefore had a Hebrew name. In Hebrew his name means "YHWH has given." YHWH is the spelling of the Name of God (see Footnote 5) and thus it is important that his name is pronounced in such a way as to maintain its original character and meaning. Many pronounce his Hebrew name as Yochanan (יוחנן) but that pronunciation loses the Name of YHWH. According to McClintock and Strong it is "a contracted form of the name JEHOHANAN." Therefore, in an effort to keep the original flavor of the name I use the Yahonatan, Yahuhanan or Yahanan when referring

to the Hebrew Disciple traditionally called John.

4 Beresheet is the transliteration of the Hebrew word בראשית which is often translated as Genesis. It means "in the beginning" and it is the name of the first book found in the Scriptures as well as the first word in that book. Keep in mind that I use the word "book" very loosely because in this modern day we use books in codex form which are bound by a spine and generally have writing on both pages. By using the word "book" we create a mental image regarding manuscripts which may not be accurate. Manuscripts such as the Torah (see Chapter 2) and other writings in the Tanak (see endnote 11) were written on scrolls, so instead of the word book, it is more accurate to refer to the scroll or the sefer (ספר) when referring to these ancient manuscripts. Therefore the "book" of Beresheet would be more accurately described as Sefer Beresheet ספר בראשית since it originally came as a scroll.

5 One of the most important revelations found within the Scriptures is the Name of God, more accurately, the Name of Elohim. Elohim (אלהים) is the proper Hebrew word which means "Mighty One." It is often translated as "God" and refers to the Creator of the Universe described in the Hebrew and Christian Scriptures. The Name of Elohim as revealed in the Hebrew Scriptures nearly 7,000 times is spelled יהוה (see Footnote 20) in Modern Hebrew. Sadly, the Name has been replaced by the ambiguous title "The LORD" in most modern English translations. This has resulted in the suppression of the Name of the Almighty to the point where most of the world has never seen or heard the Name which is intended to be known, worshipped, praised and revered by all of the Nations. The Name is linked to many prophets and particularly to The Prophet – Messiah Yahushua. A knowledge and understanding of the Name is critical to any person who considers them self to be a Believer and the subject is handled in greater detail in Book 2 of the Walk in the Light Series titled "Names."

6 Adam (אדם) was a unique creation and he was intimately related with the entire created world. His name is directly linked with the word "ground" adamah (אדמה) from which

he derives although he then received the "Breath of Life" - nishmat chayim (נשמת חיים) from Elohim. He was the special link between the Creator and the Creation and was a bridge, so to speak, between the two. The Scriptures record that he was made "in the image of Elohim" and so long as he remained obedient he could partake of the Tree of Life. He was created to live, as a complete being, forever. After the transgression in the Garden he, along with the woman Hawah (חוה), not Eve as many have been taught, were expelled and denied access to the Tree of Life. This resulted in death entering mankind, which again, was directly linked to the rest of creation. The impact was immediate although the processes of both physical and spiritual death took their own unique courses. Prior to the fall, Adam was "plugged into Elohim" spiritually. Adam could commune directly with Elohim in an intimate fashion which no created being was able to do after the fall. After being expelled he was separated from that communion. Death also began to take hold of his physical body as well of the rest of creation. Those things which were made to last forever began to die and while mankind was originally created in the image of Elohim, the offspring of Adam, beginning with Seth, were born in the image of Adam, NOT in the image of YHWH. (Beresheet 5:3). Adam contained the "breath of Life" which cannot be killed, but he existed in a body which was once eternal, but now was dying. As a result, his offspring were born in this same state.

7 Mosheh is the proper transliteration for the Hebrew name of the man commonly referred to as Moses.

8 Yisrael is the English transliteration for the Hebrew word ישראל often spelled Israel. It refers to the people of Elohim, not just to a nation in the distant past that we read about in the Scriptures, nor the Modern State of Israel. Rather, Yisrael is the Assembly of Believers who follow the Torah of Elohim.

9 While I believe in the infallibility of the Word, I do not believe in the infallibility of human translators. To do so would be to deny the obvious and actually remain in darkness. There are

many passages in the Scriptures which simply do not make sense to Believers because they have been poorly translated. These inaccurate translations often result in confusion and sometimes lead to the development of false doctrines. The example provided in Yahanan 1:17 is one simple example of this fact. There are many others discussed in the various books included in the Walk in the Light Series and this matter is particularly discussed in depth in the book entitled "Scriptures."

10 The use of the term "New Testament" gives the distinct impression that those texts have replaced the Scriptures which are commonly called the "Old Testament." This "Old" versus "New" dichotomy is consistent with the false doctrine of Replacement Theology which teaches that the "New" replaces the "Old" and that the Church is spiritual Yisrael which has replaced the Yisrael of the "Old Testament" which was physical Yisrael. These subjects will be addressed further in this discussion as well as in the Walk in the Light series book entitled "The Redeemed." The collection of writings commonly called "The New Testament" is better called The Messianic Scriptures because they describe the past and future work of the Messiah. The New Covenant, more accurately called the Renewed Covenant is found in the Tanak (see endnote 11), which is just as relevant today as the Messianic Scriptures. They fit together as a complete package and the "New" does not replace or supersede the "Old". In fact, early Believers only had the Tanak (see endnote 11) as the Messianic Scriptures were not written for decades after the resurrection of the Messiah. I believe that the Torah (see Chapter 2) is the foundation for faith in YHWH and therefore I avoid using the "Old" and "New" distinctions which tend to diminish the Tanak. This subject is described in greater detail in the Walk in the Light Series books entitled "The Scriptures" and "Covenants."

11 The Tanak is the compilation of Scriptures commonly referred to as The Hebrew Bible or The Old Testament in Christian Bibles. It consists of the Torah (Instruction), Nebi'im (Prophets) and the Kethubim (Writings), thus the

Hebrew acronym TNK which is pronounced tah-nak.

12 Quotation and previous definitions of the Ancient Semitic symbols from *Hebrew Word Pictures*, Dr. Frank T. Seekins, Living Word Pictures, Inc., Phoenix, Arizona 2003 (Elohim inserted in place of God).

13 A 12th Century Hebrew Sage named Nachmonides in his study on Beresheet Chapter 1 came to the conclusion that we live in 10 dimensions, 4 which are knowable and 6 which are unknowable. Interestingly he came to these conclusions through his study of the Torah. 20th Century Particle Physicists have reached the same conclusions. Modern science has confirmed that there are 10 dimensions – 4 which are directly measurable consisting of height, width, length and time, and 6 which are curled into less than 10^{-33} cm and therefore inferable only by indirect means. The fall of man in the Garden may have resulted in the fracture of creation dividing the 4 physical dimensions from the 6 hyper-dimensions, or spiritual dimensions.

14 Throughout the text you may find that the words "Jewish," "Jews" and "Jew" are in italics because they are ambiguous and sometimes derogatory terms. At times these expressions are used to describe all of the genetic descendants of Ya'akov (Jacob) while at other times the words describe adherents to the religion called Judaism. The terms are commonly applied to ancient Yisraelites as well as modern day descendents of those tribes, whether they are atheists or Believers in the Almighty. The word "Jew" originally referred to a member of the tribe of Yahudah (Judah) or a person that lived in the region of Judea. After the different exiles of the Kingdom of Yisrael and the Kingdom of Yahudah, it was the Yahudim that returned to the land while the House of Yisrael was scattered to the ends of the earth (Yirmeyahu (Jeremiah) 9:16). Since the Yahudim were the recognizable descendents of Ya'akov, over time with the Kingdom of Yisrael in exile, the Yahudim came to represent Yisrael and thus the term "Jew" came to represent a Yisraelite. While this label became common and customary, it is not accurate and is the cause of tremendous confusion. This subject is described in greater

detail in The Walk in the Light Series book entitled "The Redeemed."

15 The subject of the Doctrine of Dispensationalism will be discussed in more detail in Chapter 11 suffice it to say it is a very pervasive doctrine in modern Western Christianity albeit quite new.

16 Shaul (שאול) pronounced sha-ool is the proper transliteration for the Hebrew name of the apostle commonly called Paul.

17 Simply stated, Preconceived Theology is an idea or doctrine which a person is taught or believes to be true without necessarily being based upon the Scriptures. Often times a person learns from their friends, parents or pastor before they read the Scriptures. This inevitably happens to all people because they typically go to Sunday School before they become Bible Scholars. As a result of all of this conditioning that we receive from various sources as we grow up – if and when we finally endeavor to read and study the Scriptures - we do so with many of our belief systems already in place. This sometimes results in an interpretation of Scriptures in such a way as to fit within the paradigm constructed by our preexisting belief rather than the actual meaning of the Scriptures. It is critical that we strip away any doctrines which do not agree with the Scriptures but this is sometimes difficult when the Scriptures have already been filtered through someone else's (ie. translator's) preconceived theology. Thus the need to get back to the roots of the faith and the most accurate transcripts of the Scriptures so that we can glean their original intent and meaning.

18 The term "Old Testament" is often used to describe the Scriptures commonly known as the "Jewish Bible" or the Tanak. I believe that the term "Old Testament" is terribly misleading because it gives the impression that everything contained therein is old or outdated. While growing up in a mainline Christian denomination I was given the distinct impression that it was full of great stories, but it applied to "The Jews" and was ultimately replaced by the "New Testament" which contained the important Scriptures for Christians. While this may or may not have been done

intentionally, I believe that it is a notion which is pervasive throughout much of the Christian religion. Without a doubt the Tanak, and in particular, the Torah are essential to the faith and these are the Scriptures which must be at the core of every person's belief system. If these truths are not at the foundation and considered completely relevant for today, then people are prone to be misled and follow false and twisted doctrines. This matter is discussed at length in the Walk in the Light Series book entitled "Scriptures."

19 This is where Christianity goes afoul. History reveals men such as Marcion who taught that the "God" of the "Old Testament" is different than the "God" of the "New Testament." The impression given is that the "new" is better than the "old" and that the "new" has even replaced the "old." This is a very dangerous teaching and - needless to say – false and has led to such other erroneous distinctions as that made between Yisrael and "The Church." The word "church" is a man-made word which is typically associated with the Catholic and Christian religions. In that context it is meant to describe the corporate body of faith. It is used in most modern English Bibles as a translation for the Greek word ekklesia (εκκλεσια) which simply means "assembly." It does not necessarily have any religious connotation as can be seen in Acts 19:39-41 where the word ekklesia was used to refer to the courts and also the riotous mob that was accusing some of the disciples. When applied to Believers it refers to the "called out assembly of YHWH." The word "church" derives from pagan origins, namely the name Circe – the daughter of Helios, and its misuse is part of the problem associated with Replacement Theology which teaches that the "Church" has replaced Yisrael, which in Hebrew is called the qahal (קהל): "the called out assembly of YHWH." The Hebrew *qahal* and Greek *ekklesia* therefore represent the same thing when referring to Believers: The Commonwealth of Yisrael. Therefore, the continued use of the word "church" is divisive, confusing and simply incorrect. This subject is described in greater detail in the Walk in the Light Series book entitled "The Redeemed."

20 YHWH (יהוה) is the four letter Name of the Elohim described in the Scriptures. This four letter Name has commonly been called the "Tetragrammaton" and traditionally it has been considered to be ineffable or unpronounceable. As a result, despite the fact that it is found nearly 7,000 times in the Hebrew Scriptures, it has been replaced with such titles as "The Lord," "Adonai" and "HaShem." I believe that this practice is in direct violation of the First and Third Commandments. Some commonly accepted pronunciations are: Yahweh, Yahuwah and Yahowah. Since there is debate over which pronunciation is correct I simply use the Name as it is found in the Scriptures, although I spell it in English from left to right, rather than in Hebrew from right to left. For the person who truly desires to know the nature of the Elohim described in the Scriptures, a good place to start is the Name by which He revealed Himself to all mankind.

21 Kepha is the proper transliteration for the Hebrew name of the disciple commonly called Peter.

22 Yahrushalayim is a transliteration of the word commonly pronounced as Jerusalem. Since there in no "J" in Hebrew it would be impossible that the actual name of the city was Jerusalem. Since it is a City where YHWH will place His Name (2 Chronicles 33:4) it only makes sense that it would include the poetic short form of the Name "Yah."

23 The Feasts of YHWH, also called the Appointed Times or moadim never belonged to the "Jews" and contrary to popular belief, they are not the "Jewish" Holidays. Rather they belong to YHWH as specifically stated in Vayiqra 23:4. They are times for all who serve YHWH to celebrate. This subject is dealt with at length in the Walk in the Light series book entitled "The Appointed Times."

24 Yisraelites were not only direct descendents of the Twelve Tribes of Yisrael, but also Gentile converts. This entire Commonwealth of Yisrael was divided into different groups and followed different doctrines and lifestyles. While this is not the ultimate desire of YHWH that His people be divided, it is what happens when men stray from the truth like sheep without a shepherd. (Mattityahu 9:36). The early Believers

of Yahushua were a sect of Yisrael that believed that He was the Messiah. This remained until such time as Christianity became a new and separate religion apart from Yisrael.

25 *Antiquities of the Jews* 12.10.6 (13.297), Josephus Flavius, [Whiston Translation p. 281].

26 *The Hebrew Yeshua vs. the Greek Jesus*, Nehemia Gordon, Hilkiah Press (2005).

27 For a good treatment of the rise of Rabbinic Judaism I recommend the book *Rabbi Akiba's Messiah: The Origins of Rabbinic Authority* by Daniel Grubner, Elijah Publishing (1999).

28 *Ibid* Gordon, Nehemia, Appendix 3, Page 83.

29 *Jewish New Testament Commentary*, David H. Stern, Jewish New Testament Publications, Inc. (1992) Page 25 (The use of Elohim and the spelling of Yahushua conformed for consistency by this author).

30 The mikvah is where the Christian doctrine of baptism derives although it did not begin with Christianity and was commanded by YHWH long before Messiah came. It was a natural thing for Yisraelites to do - in fact there were hundreds of mikvahs at the temple and it was required that a person be immersed in a mikvah prior to presenting their sacrifice. The Hebrew word for baptize is tevila (טביל) which is a full body immersion that takes place in a mikvah (מקוה) which comes from the passage in Beresheet 1:10 when YHWH "gathered together" the waters. The mikvah is the gathering together of flowing waters. The "tevila" immersion is symbolic for a person going from a state of uncleanliness to cleanliness. The priests in the temple needed to tevila regularly to insure that they were in a state of cleanliness when they served in the Temple. Anyone going to the Temple to worship or offer sacrifices would tevila at the numerous pools outside the Temple. There are a variety of instances found in the Torah when a person was required to tevila. It is very important because it reminds us of the filth of sin and the need to be washed clean from our sin in order to stand in the presence of a holy, set apart Elohim. Therefore it makes perfect sense that we be immersed in a

mikvah prior to presenting the sacrifice of the perfect lamb as atonement for our sins. It also cleanses our temple which the Spirit of Elohim will enter in to tabernacle with us. The tevila is symbolic of becoming born again and is an act of going from one life to another. Being born again is not something that became popular in the seventies within the Christian religion. It is a remarkably Yisraelite concept that was understood to occur when one arose from the mikvah. In fact people witnessing an immersion would often cry out "Born Again!" when a person came up from an immersion. It was also an integral part of the Rabbinic conversion process, which, in many ways is not Scriptural, but in this sense is correct. For a Gentile to complete their conversion, they were required to be immersed, or baptized, which meant that they were born again: born into a new life. Many people fail to realize that this concept is not a Christian concept because of the exchange between Messiah and Nicodemus. Let us take a look at that conversation in the Gospel according to Yahanan: "[1] *Now there was a man of the Pharisees named Nicodemus, a ruler of the Yahudim.* [2] *He came to Yahushua at night and said, 'Rabbi, we know you are a teacher who has come from Elohim. For no one could perform the miraculous signs you are doing if Elohim were not with him.'* [3] *In reply Yahushua declared, 'I tell you the truth, no one can see the kingdom of Elohim unless he is born again.'* [4] *'How can a man be born when he is old?' Nicodemus asked. 'Surely he cannot enter a second time into his mother's womb to be born!'* [5] *Yahushua answered, 'I tell you the truth, no one can enter the kingdom of Elohim unless he is born of water and the Spirit.* [6] *Flesh gives birth to flesh, but the Spirit gives birth to spirit.* [7] *You should not be surprised at my saying, You must be born again.* [8] *The wind blows wherever it pleases. You hear its sound, but you cannot tell where it comes from or where it is going. So it is with everyone born of the Spirit.'* [9] *'How can this be?' Nicodemus asked.* [10] *'You are Yisrael's teacher,' said Yahushua, 'and do you not understand these things?* [11] *I tell you the truth, we speak of what we know, and we testify to what we have seen, but still you people do not accept our testimony.* [12] *I have spoken to you of earthly things and you do not believe; how then will you believe if I speak of heavenly things?* [13] *No one has ever gone into heaven except the one who came from heaven-the Son of Man.* [14] *Just as Mosheh lifted up the snake in the desert, so the Son of Man must be lifted up,* [15] *that everyone who believes in him may have eternal life.'"* Yahanan 3:1-15. Nicodemus was not surprised by the fact that a person needed to be "born again." His first question: "*How can a man be born when he is old?*" demonstrated he did not see how it applied to him, because he was already a Yahudim. His second question "*How can this be,*" only affirmed that fact. And this is why Yahushua said: "*You are Yisrael's teacher and do you not understand these things.*" In other words, "you're supposed to be the one teaching Yisrael about these spiritual matters and you're not. You think only the Gentiles need to be immersed and born again, but you all need it because you are all sinners and this needs to be taught to everyone, not just the Gentiles." This is why Yahanan the Immerser (John the Baptist) had been immersing Yisraelites in preparation for the Messiah. So you see, being born again through immersion was not new to Yisrael, this is why many readily were immersed by Yahanan the Immerser - they understood their need. It was often the leaders who failed to see their need for cleansing because they were blinded by the notion that their Torah observance justified them. It is important to note that the tevila must occur in "living waters" - in other words, water which is moving and ideally which contains life. These living waters refer to the Messiah. In a Scriptural marriage, a bride would enter the waters of purification prior to her wedding. These are the same waters that we are to enter when we make a confession of faith and become part of the Body of Messiah - His Bride. A bride also enters the waters of separation when her niddah period has ended so that she can be reunited with her husband. Oral tradition requires approximately 200 gallons of water in order to qualify as a mikvah.

31 There is something even more profound here than the defiance of a Pharisaic Tradition. The fact that we are told the specific quantity of water which the jugs could hold (approximately 180 gallons) it is evident that these stone jugs were used for

a mikvah. The fact that the scene is a wedding feast points directly to the picture of a bride becoming ritually pure to join physically with her husband. The fact that Yahushua used those pots which were supposed to provide cleansing to the Bride and filled them with water which then became wine is an incredible picture of the work of the Messiah. At the Last Supper He declared that the wine symbolized His Blood which should take us back to the miracle of turning water into wine. It speaks of the cleansing power of His blood and as the Waters of Life cleanse a bride so the Blood of Messiah cleanses His Bride. This subject is a book in and of itself and I encourage the reader to contemplate upon this miracle which has much more significance than some "magic trick" of turning water into wine as so many simplistically perceive the event at Cana.

32 Talmud - Mas. Shabbath 108b "[To put] wine into one's eye is forbidden; [to put it] on the eye, is permitted. Whilst the other said: [To put] tasteless saliva, even on the eye, is forbidden."

33 The healing of a leper was no random act – it was intentional and symbolic – just as the healing of the blind, the lame, the deaf and the dumb and raising the dead. These were all things that the Messiah was prophesied to do concerning the House of Ya'akov (Jacob). That is why Yahushua instructed the disciples of Yahanan the Immerser as follows: "[22] *Yahushua answered and said to them, 'Go and tell Yahanan the things you have seen and heard: that the blind see, the lame walk, the lepers are cleansed, the deaf hear, the dead are raised, the poor have the good news preached to them.* [23] *And blessed is he who is not offended because of Me.*" Luke 7:22-23. These were all signs of the Messiah.

34 Mitzvot is the Hebrew word for Commandment and the mitzvot pertaining specifically to a person healed of leprosy is found in Vayiqra 14:1-32. It is very detailed and some said that this was so detailed because it was a sign of the Messiah. When a person appeared to perform this mitzvot it would alert the priests that the Messiah or a great Prophet had

arrived.

35 The religious leaders had developed 39 primary categories of work which was prohibited on the Sabbath along with numerous subcategories. They most likely defined the actions of the disciples as falling in the category of reaping.

36 http://www.beingjewish.com/shabbat/washing.html

37 A good example of the difference between the "yoke" of the Torah and the "yoke" of the Pharisees can be seen regarding the Sabbath. While the Torah only has a few specific commands concerning the Sabbath, the Takanot of the Pharisees and the Rabbis consists of hundreds, if not thousands of rules and regulations. The yoke of the Torah is light and is meant to guide us in the paths of righteousness while the yoke of men becomes a burden that few, if any, can bear.

38 There are clearly those servants who speak and teach the truth who do so with legitimate authority. The Temple service also had very explicit regulations and there were certain functions that only the Levites, Cohens or High Priest could perform. Ultimately when we are talking about assembling together and worship there is a need for order and it is perfectly fine that individuals are given the authority to coordinate and serve the assembly. The important distinction is that those servants do not have the authority to "rule over" the individuals that they are serving. Each and every Believer has the opportunity to commune with the Creator and receive instruction directly from Him. That is what He wants and He does not like men, particularly religious "leaders" sticking their noses where they do not belong. It always bothered me to observe people running to the Pastor, Priest or Rabbi whenever they had a problem instead of running to their High Priest - Yahushua. While fellowship is important and we have much to learn from our brethren, it is a bad habit to get into.

39 Rabbinic Judaism has a long history of working against the ministry and even the Name of Yahushua. While Judaism is not known for evangelism and even encourages people against converting, there is an active group known as "Anti-missionaries" who seek to counter the teachings

of Christianity and any other system or teaching which involves Messiah Yahushua.

40 This translation corrects most modern English translations which derive from the accepted Greek text. The Hebrew and Aramaic texts provide a much more consistent and clearer understanding of the teaching of Yahushua which has baffled many Bible Scholars for centuries. The existence of the Hebrew Matthew is undisputed and many early Believers wrote about the fact that Mattityahu (Matthew) wrote his account in Hebrew. Papias a disciple of Yahanan (ca 60-130 CE) wrote: "[Mattityahu] collected the Oracles in the Hebrew Language, and each interpreted them as best he could." It was also referred to by Irenaeus, Origen quoted by Eusebius and Eusebius. *Hebrew Gospel of Matthew*, George Howard, Mercer University Press, 1995, pp. 155-160.

41 Mattityahu is the proper transliteration for the name of the Hebrew disciple commonly called Matthew. His name means: "Gift of Yah."

42 Rabbinowitz, Noel S., *Matthew 23:2-4: Does Jesus Recognize the Authority of the Pharisees and Does He Endorse Their Halakah?* Journal of the Evangelical Theological Society JETS 46/3 (Sept. 2003) pp. 423-47.

43 Examining the parallels between Mosheh and Yahushua is truly a study in and of itself although it is worth commenting that both started out their lives in the humblest of beginnings Mosheh in an Ark and Yahushua in a Sukkah, or Manger. Both the Ark and the Sukkah symbolize the covering or protection of YHWH and have profound spiritual significance. While Mosheh was described as "*very humble more than all men who were on the face of the earth*" (Bemidbar 12:3) he was also like a "god." (Shemot 4:16). So too Yahushua was humble (Mattityahu 11:29) and He stated "*he who has seen Me has seen the Father*" Yahanan 14:9. Both were adopted into their earthly father's family - Mosheh into the House of Pharaoh and Yahushua into the House of Yoseph. While the Scriptures reveal that Yahushua came from the Seed of YHWH, they do not immediately reveal the seed from which Mosheh came - thus an absence of an Earthly Father

– this of course, is no coincidence. They both spent time in the desert, they both spent time on the mountain, they both mediated the marriage between YHWH and His people Yisrael. They both taught the Torah and interestingly, where Mosheh left off after Redeeming Yisrael by the Hand of YHWH, his protégé Yahushua (Joshua) picked up and circumcised the people and led them into the promised Land by the Hand of YHWH. Again the patterns could not be any clearer for us to follow. The Messiah in His dual role as suffering servant (Yeshayahu 53) and conquering King (Jeremiah (Yirmeyahu) 23:5-6) will function in both of these roles.

44 The "book" of Deuteronomy would be more accurately described as Sefer Devarim ספר דברים since it originally came as a scroll. Devarim means "words" in Hebrew.

45 What happened at Mt. Sinai was a marriage ceremony between YHWH and His Bride – Yisrael. After delivering her from bondage He then gave her the opportunity to become His Bride - if she agreed to obey the Torah. The Torah was, in essence, a marriage contract or a ketubah. The people declared: "*All that YHWH has spoken we will do.*" Shemot 19:8. In other words, "I Do" or rather "We Do." They agreed to the marriage and were commanded to prepare for the marriage ceremony by cleansing and consecrating themselves. After hearing the Ten Commandments they could not take it anymore and asked Mosheh to relay the Words of YHWH. Mosheh ascended the mountain while the people waited and ultimately got impatient. They decided to make up their own celebration to YHWH and create a golden calf, just as they had seen in Mitsrayim (Egypt). They had already been instructed not to make any images and if they had only waited and listened a bit further, they would have heard the instruction regarding an altar and the prohibition against gold and silver gods which was commanded immediately after the 10th commandment. Regardless, they committed adultery before they even consummated the marriage. In very crude terms, it was like a bride excusing herself during the wedding feast and having sex with an old boyfriend while

the groom is waiting for her to go on their honeymoon. It was understandably infuriating to YHWH. As a result, the covenant was broken, and Mosheh literally broke the Tablets which contained the covenant. Mosheh thereafter went up to YHWH to make atonement (Shemot 32:30). The covenant was later renewed and placed upon new tablets, this time cut by Mosheh instead of YHWH which provided a vivid picture of the Messiah and the future renewed covenant, although the terms were written by YHWH and remained the same - the Torah. The desire of YHWH is for His Bride to know Him. In fact, you must "know YHWH" to be married to Him and this "knowledge" is much more than a handshake or friendly introduction. The Hebrew word for know is yada (ידע) which has a variety of meanings but in this context means intimate relations. The example which is provided through the Scriptures is the intimate "knowledge" shared between a husband and a wife. While YHWH was always a faithful Husband to His Bride, Yisrael was not always a faithful bride. She went whoring and the House of Yisrael was actually divorced from YHWH. As a result, before the restorative work of YHWH can be completed, He must renew the covenant with Yisrael, His Bride - not the Church.

46 The plan of YHWH is laid out through His covenants - none of which have been abolished or done away with as is often taught in Christianity. The so-called "Old Covenant" found in the Tanak was the process of restoring mankind from his fallen state to a Redeemed people called Yisrael who would be a Kingdom of Priests that would obey YHWH and exercise dominion over the earth as Adam was intended to do. Since Yisrael was divided and subsequently both the House of Yisrael and the House of Yahudah broke the covenant, it needed to be renewed. Just as the original covenant involved the Torah, so too the Renewed Covenant involved the Torah – only when it was renewed it would be written on our hearts and minds instead of on tablets of stone. Read what the Prophet Yirmeyahu (Jeremiah) proclaims: "31 *Behold, the days are coming, says YHWH, when I will make a renewed covenant*

with the house of Yisrael and with the house of Yahudah — [32] *not according to the covenant that I made with their fathers in the day that I took them by the hand to lead them out of the land of Egypt, My covenant which they broke, though I was a husband to them, says YHWH.* [33] *But this is the covenant that I will make with the house of Yisrael after those days, says YHWH: I will put My Torah in their minds, and write it on their hearts; and I will be their Elohim, and they shall be My people.* [34] *No more shall every man teach his neighbor, and every man his brother, saying, 'Know YHWH,' for they all shall know Me, from the least of them to the greatest of them, says YHWH. For I will forgive their iniquity, and their sin I will remember no more."* Yirmeyahu 31:31-34. The subject of covenants is described in greater detail in the Walk in the Light series entitled "Covenants."

47 Yirmeyahu (ירמיהו) is the proper transliteration for the Hebrew name of the prophet commonly called Jeremiah.

48 The Shema, also known as The Sh'ma is often considered to be a prayer, but as Messiah pointed out, it is the First Command which declares: "[4] Hear, O Yisrael: YHWH our Elohim, YHWH is one! [5] You shall love YHWH your Elohim with all your heart, with all your soul, and with all your strength." Devarim 6:4-5. This command is found in the Tanak although Yahushua continues to teach that it is the First Command. This flies directly in the face of those who argue that Messiah did away with the Torah or changed the Torah, that of course is both absurd and impossible.

49 A bondservant is the relationship which exists when an individual decides to serve and follow another. The Scriptures depict a person who was a slave or servant and entitled to their freedom in the seventh (Sabbath) year, but because of the love that they have for their Master they willingly submit to serve Him and become a part of His household forever. (Shemot 21:1-6). Many of the early disciples described themselves as bondservants including Shaul and Timotheos (Philippians 1:1; Titus 1:1, Romans 1:1), Epaphras (Colossians 4:12), James (Ya'akov 1:1), Shimon Kepha (2 Kepha 1:1) and Jude (Yahudah 1). Even the Messiah was described as taking the form of a Bondservant (Philippians 2:7).

50 It is important to understand the difference between justice and mercy. If you are looking for justice all of the time you may get justice in return, but that may not be what you want. You see, we are all deserving of death because we have all intentionally transgressed the Torah at one time or another. Therefore if you want justice, which is something that you deserve, then you can have it - which is death. I prefer mercy - getting something which I do not deserve. Likewise, Yahushua is instructing His followers to be like YHWH - Who is patient and rich in mercy - when dealing with others.

51 The Essenes were one of many different Sects of Yisraelites that existed during the time of Yahushua. There is much speculation concerning whether they were a monastic group based at Qumran on the northern end of the Dead Sea or whether they were, in fact, living in an amongst the greater assembly of Yisrael. Much insight into their teachings and beliefs has been gained since the discovery of The Dead Sea Scrolls which also gives us greater insight into the teachings of Yahushua as he was probably referencing an Essene text which stated "...bear unremitting hatred towards all men of ill repute... to leave it to them to pursue wealth and mercenary gain... truckling to a depot."(Man. Of Disc. Ix, 21-26).

52 The American Heritage Dictionary.

53 *The Jewish Book of Why*, Alfred J. Kolatch, Penguin Group (2000) p.173.

54 The Appointed Times described in Vayiqra 23, as well as other portions of the Torah, are often erroneously referred to as the Jewish Holidays. This is a grave mistake because YHWH specifically says that these are "My appointed times." They belong to no ethnic or religious group. This topic is discussed in greater detail in the Walk in the Light series book entitled "Appointed Times." For the purposes of this discussion it is important to point out that the Feast of Pentecost takes place 49 days after the Feast of Firstfruits which occurs during the Feast of Unleavened Bread. Pentecost, also known as Shavuot (weeks) is one of three feasts when all males are commanded to go up to Yahrushalayim. While at the Feast you would

go to the Temple, or rather House of YHWH, for prayer and offerings, particularly during the morning (9:00 am) and evening (3:00 pm also known as the 9th hour). Contrary to popular belief, on the day of Pentecost, the Disciples were not huddled in the upper room, which was no doubt quite small. Rather they were in the House of YHWH at 9:00 am for the Feast. This is how such a crowd from around the world could gather to witness the outpouring and the speaking in many languages. These were all of the Torah observant Yisraelites who were present for the Feast. The Scriptures record that 3,000 were added to the faith and baptized, or rather immersed. There were hundreds of mikvahs at the Temple where people would cleanse themselves before entering the House of YHWH, this is how they were able to immerse so many people.

55 In an effort not to violate any of the commandments, the Rabbis and their predecessors "built a fence" around the Torah, which means that they developed a new set of regulations intended to keep people far away from violating any of the commandments. While this may seem like a noble endeavor, it is really quite presumptuous and a clear violation of the Torah when it involves adding to the Torah, which is often exactly what happens. As a result, men start learning, studying and obeying the man-made regulations which then diminish and supersede the clear instructions found within the Torah itself.

56 There are 14 writings attributed to Shaul although considerable speculation exists in the academic community as to the authorship of epistles such as Ephesians, Colossians, 2 Thessalonians, Titus, I Timothy, 2 Timothy and Hebrews to name some of them. In fact, Origen (ca 182 – ca 251 CE), despite the problems concerning his Platonic influenced doctrine, specifically stated that Shaul did not write the Letter to the Hebrews and only God knows who did. The reasons for the speculation vary from the doctrinal content to the actual writing styles. It is also believed that there were many other letters that he wrote which have been lost. The point is that Shaul was a man, he was a teacher and a missionary.

He was also a scholar well taught regarding the Torah. I do not believe that he wrote his letters with the intention that they be treated as Scripture. In fact, if he saw how people regard his letters, sometimes greater than the Torah and the teachings of Messiah, he would probably roll over in his tomb.

57 Shaul rightly understood that it was the circumcision of the heart which was performed by the Messiah and which was integral to the Renewed Covenant. The prophet Yirmeyahu addressed the issue centuries prior. "[25] *The days are coming, declares YHWH, when I will punish all who are circumcised only in the flesh-* [26] *Mitsrayim, Yahudah, Edom, Ammon, Moab and all who live in the desert in distant places. For all these nations are really uncircumcised, and even the whole house of Yisrael is uncircumcised in heart.*" Jeremiah 9:25-26. It was through Shaul's efforts to explain this important truth that often resulted in him being branded as teaching against the Torah.

58 The correct Hebrew name of the half brother of Yahushua, often called James, is Ya'akov.

59 The Christian religion spends so much time focusing on the Apostle Shaul that they often neglect the fact that Ya'akov, the half brother of Messiah, was the undisputed leader of the Yahrushalayim Assembly of Believers which was obviously the center of the faith of Yisrael. He and the elders gave instructions to Shaul and the writings of Ya'akov concerning the Torah are clear and unambiguous. I would recommend that anyone examine the writings of Ya'akov for a solid analysis of the relationship between the Torah and grace.

60 The road to Damascus experience was not a conversion as many like to describe it. Shaul did not convert to Christianity as Christianity did not even exist for hundreds of years after that time. Contrary to popular belief, the Christian religion is not the same faith as that which was practiced by the first talmidim of the Messiah and Yisrael. All of the original talmidim were Yisraelites and all of the original Believers were Yisraelites. Early Gentile converts were "grafted in" to the Olive Tree which represents The Commonwealth

of Yisrael (Romans 11). Over the decades and centuries that followed the death and resurrection of Messiah, pagan doctrines and anti-Semitism infiltrated and divided the Assembly of Believers. The historical persecution of the Yisraelites by the Roman Empire led to the demise of the Yisraelite Believers (commonly called Nazoreans) and the surge of Christianity, which perpetrated the concept that "The Church" had replaced the Elect of Elohim, which is Yisrael. The Christian Religion was officially established by the Roman Empire in the Third Century by Emperor Constantine – a pagan who worshipped the sun god Mithra. By that time there had been a significant departure from the original faith presented in the Scriptures by Avraham, Yitshaq, Ya'akov, Mosheh, the Prophets and the Messiah. The new religion called Christianity was a mixture of the truth, anti-Semitism and sun god worship which has twisted and distorted Scriptures for centuries to become a religion of lawlessness that, in many ways, stands diametrically opposed to the will and commandments of Elohim. Therefore, Shaul never converted to anything. He remained a Yisraelite who stopped persecuting followers of Yahushua because he realized that Yahushua was indeed the Messiah. Once he got straightened out he then traveled to teach this truth to others.

61 Eliyahu is the correct transliteration of the Hebrew name for the prophet of Yisrael commonly called Elijah. The name means: "YHWH is Elohim."

62 Few people realize the continuing significance of Sinai throughout the Scriptures. This is the place where the Torah was given through Mosheh to the nation of Yisrael. It is also the place where Eliyahu fled, a forty day journey, in one day and met with the Word of YHWH. (1 Kings 19:8-9). While the traditional location of Mount Sinai has been in the Sinai Peninsula there is overwhelming archeological evidence pointing to Saudi Arabia. Beyond the physical evidence it certainly concurs with Shaul going to Sinai as he comments in Galatians 1:17 of going to Arabia after his encounter with Yahushua on the road to Damascus. Mattityahu 4:1-11 recounts the wilderness experience of Yahushua and refers

to an exceedingly high mountain which I believe could have been Horeb (Sinai).

63 The word Gentile is thrown around a lot as if a person in that group is the member of another species - when in fact a Gentile was simply someone who was not part of the Commonwealth of Yisrael. Some other words used to describe this category of people were: Heathens, Goyim or Nations. They were those who did not worship the Holy One of Yisrael and instead, worshipped false gods, or none at all. If you followed YHWH you joined with Yisrael and you were a Yisraelite - you did not convert to Judaism. While Judaism is an offshoot of Yisrael it is very different from the Yisrael described in the Tanak. Therefore, Shaul was ministering to the Gentiles in order to draw them into the Kingdom of Yisrael – not any particular religion or denomination.

64 Canonization is a man-made concept which determines whether certain writings are accepted as Scripture and therefore included in the Bible. The canonization of the modern day Bible took place at the Council of Laodicea in Phrygia Pacatiana somewhere between 343 A.D and 381 A.D. A commonly accepted date is 364 A.D. although no one can say for certain when the Synod took place. This subject is addressed in detail in the Walk in the Light Series book entitled "Scriptures."

65 The Greek word that is often translated as "cross" in English translations of the Scriptures is stauron (σταυρόν) which means "stake" or "pole". The word cross has traditionally been inserted to support the iconic worship of the crucifix which derives from the ancient Tao (X) which was traditionally used in sun god worship long before Christianity was established. The tau stood for Tammuz the Babylonian sun god who was killed by a wild boar resulting in a 40 day period of weeping for Tammuz which the Catholics call Lent. The eating of ham on Easter Sunday is also a tradition derived from sun god worship since Easter, a pagan goddess also known as Astarte, Ishtar and Sameramus among others, was the Queen of Heaven, and mother of Tammuz.

66 Dawid (דוד) is a proper transliteration for the Hebrew name

commonly called David.

67 Yirmeyahu is the proper transliteration for the prophet commonly called Jeremiah. His name means: "Yah will lift up or exalt".

68 Ibrim or Ivrim is a proper transliteration for the word Hebrews.

69 This is why context is so important – particularly when reading the Epistles in the Messianic Scriptures. When you are reading a letter from Shaul, you are often times only reading a portion of a controversy and if you do not understand the issue that he is addressing, it would be easy to misinterpret or misapply his teachings.

70 As mentioned previously, Rabbinic Judaism is not the same religion as that of the Yisrael that we read in the Scriptures. Rabbinic Judaism is a religion which was developed largely because of the Great Revolt. After the siege on Jerusalem and the destruction of the Second Temple by Titus in 70 A.D., the Pharisees and possibly only surviving Sanhedrin member Yochanan ben Zakkai founded an Academy at Yavneh which became the center of Rabbinic Authority. His successor Gamaliel II continued to solidify the power base of the Pharisaic Sect of the Hebrews who, through their cooperation with the Roman Empire, were able to survive the near annihilation which was suffered by the other Yisraelite sects such as the Sadducees, the Essenes, the Zealots, the Sicarii and the Nazoreans. There were still other sects of Yisraelites which history provides scant detail such as the Therapeutae and those who composed the "Odes of Solomon." In any event, the Pharisees, through the enhancement of Rabbinic authority and the leadership of Rabbi Akiba developed into the leading Yisraelite sect which is now known as Rabbinic Judaism. While Rabbinic Judaism claims to stem directly from Yisrael it is not much different from the Roman Catholic church claiming a direct line of "Popes" to Shimon Kepha. These claims of authority are quite meaningless as neither religious system represents the pure faith found in the Scriptures. Rabbinic Judaism, while it may consist of mostly genetic descendents of Avraham,

Yitshaq and Ya'akov, is not Yisrael. In other words, you do not have to convert to Judaism to become part of the Commonwealth of Yisrael (ie. the Kingdom of Elohim) nor do you have to accept Talmudic teaching to follow Elohim. Rabbinic Judaism does not have a Temple nor a priesthood and their Rabbinic power structure is not supported or condoned by the Scriptures. This is why the Talmud, which is not Scripture, is so important in Rabbinic Judaism, because it lends credence to their newly devised system. When the Messiah returns He will set things straight. He will find and lead His sheep and He will not need any Catholic Priests, Christian Pastors or Jewish Rabbis to help Him.

71 Egypt is the modern word used to describe the land inhabited by the descendents of Mitsrayim, who was the son of Ham (Beresheet 10:6). Thus, throughout this text the word Mitsrayim will be used in place of the English word Egypt since that is how it is rendered in the Torah.

72 Pesach is the proper Hebrew word for the Appointed time commonly called Passover. It is one of three Feasts where all male Yisraelite are required to gather and celebrate in Yahrushalayim. The appointed times are discussed in detail in the Walk in the Light series book entitled "Appointed Times."

73 Yeshayahu (ישעיהו) is the proper transliteration for the Prophet commonly called Isaiah. His name in Hebrew means "YHWH saves."

74 It cannot be stressed enough that there is no act that man can do to make himself justified before YHWH. It is by faith alone that a person is saved, but that is not where it ends. That person must then live a life which is acceptable to YHWH and that life is found in His instructions - His Torah.

75 Contrary to popular belief America is not a Democracy - it is a Federal Republic. Instead of a democratic system where majority rules, in the United States, the majority elects representatives who govern on behalf of all of their constituents. The American governmental system is quite remarkable but sadly, with the passage of time, the rights

and freedoms which so many citizens enjoyed, and fought and died for, over the centuries have diminished to the point where the freedom that we talk about, to a large extent, is an illusion. The privacy rights and liberties which were so unique and fundamental to American society have been stripped away, particularly over the past century, to the point where I believe the Founding Fathers would probably be in shock at how quickly the nation has deteriorated. A once proud and diligent populace has been lulled into a dream state and have become like cattle that go out to pasture and chew the cud until "milking time." People have become so focused on the "American Dream" of a house, two cars, nicely mowed lawn, an annual trip to Disney World and a retirement plan that they failed to see the shackles of slavery that were placed upon them while they were busily pursuing their dream. Obviously, I am being a bit facetious but I am deadly serious. The America that we see today is fundamentally different than the America of a century ago. Modern Americans have traded their freedom for the promise of security. They value the comfort of their existence more than their freedoms to the point that they do not even have the stomach to wage war if it means a significant loss of life will be involved. Therefore while the number of laws in a particular nation do not necessarily correlate to the level of freedom, if the citizens of a nation, kingdom or religious system fail to diligently "guard" (shamar) their constitution or Torah, the Nicolaitans will inevitably attempt to take control and rule over the masses. Just as American citizens are charged to defend the constitution against tyranny - even when the tyrant is their own government - so followers of YHWH must guard the Torah from religious tyrants who attempt to take away the liberties and freedoms provided therein.

76 The word "church" is a man-made word generally associated with the Catholic and Christian religions. In that context it is typically meant to describe the corporate body of faith. It is used in most modern English Bibles as a translation for the Greek word ekklesia (εκκλεσια) which generally refers to the "called out assembly of YHWH." The word

"church" derives from pagan origins and its misuse is part of the problem associated with Replacement Theology which teaches that the "Church" has replaced Yisrael, which in Hebrew is called the qahal (קהל): "the called out assembly of YHWH." The Hebrew "qahal" and Greek "ekklesia" are the same thing: The Commonwealth of Yisrael. Therefore, the continued use of the word "church" is divisive and confusing. It gives the impression that the "church" is something new or different from Yisrael. This subject is described in greater detail in The Walk in the Light Series book entitled "The Redeemed."

77 The word "Bible" is placed in quotes because while it has been traditionally used to describe the collection or documents considered by Christianity to be inspired by Elohim, I prefer the use of the word Scriptures. The word Bible derives from Byblos which has more pagan connotations than I prefer, especially when referring to the written Word of Elohim. This subject is discussed in greater detail in the Walk in the Light Series book entitled "Scriptures."

78 "The Orthodox and Chasidim typically use the word 'shul,' which is Yiddish. The word is derived from a German word meaning "school," and emphasizes the synagogue's role as a place of study. Conservative Jews usually use the word "synagogue," which is actually a Greek translation of Beit K'nesset and means "place of assembly" (it's related to the word "synod"). Reform Jews use the word "temple," because they consider every one of their meeting places to be equivalent to, or a replacement for, The Temple." www.shomairyisrael.org.

79 Sadly, not only does Christianity encourage Gentiles to avoid the Torah but so does Judaism. In fact, many "Jews" would tell you that a Gentile cannot and should not obey the Torah because Rabbinic Judaism has developed a false teaching that the Torah is only for "Jews" and they define what it means to be a "Jew." They also teach that Gentiles are only subject to what has been coined the "7 Noahide Laws" which they some how construe from Genesis 9. (Sanhedrin 56a; Rambam, Hil. Melachim 9:1). You can look for them but

you will not find them. This is a Rabbinic creation which is meant to keep Gentiles away from the Torah. How sad that Yisrael is supposed to shine as a light to the Nations and draw people to YHWH while Judaism, which purports to be descended from Yisrael, often times does just the opposite.

80 *The Didache*, Chapter 6:6, J.B. Lightfoot English Translation, www.earlychristianwritings.com.

81 *Matthew Henry's Commentary on the Whole Bible*: New Modern Edition, Electronic Database. Copyright (c) 1991 by Hendrickson Publishers, Inc. [Names and titles corrected for conformity].

82 Christianity and Judaism both contain pagan elements. Christianity has rejected the Scriptural Appointed Times and has adopted pagan holidays such as Christmas and Easter. Christianity has rejected the seventh day Sabbath and replaced it with SunDay worship - the traditional day for sun worship. These issues and many others are discussed throughout the Walk in the Light series including "Restoration," "The Sabbath," "Appointed Times" and "Pagan Holidays."

83 The subject of the Scriptural dietary instructions is discussed in detail in the Walk in the Light series book entitled "Kosher."

84 The Messianic Scriptures actually state that "Jesus declared all foods clean" but this particular passage does not provide for the abolition of the dietary instructions as so many believe. Let us take a closer look at the passage in the Good News according to Mark from the NIV Translation. "[14] *Again Jesus called the crowd to Him and said, 'Listen to Me, everyone, and understand this.* [15] *Nothing outside a man can make him unclean by going into him. Rather, it is what comes out of a man that makes him unclean.'* [17] *After he had left the crowd and entered the house, his disciples asked him about this parable.* [18] *'Are you so dull?' he asked. 'Don't you see that nothing that enters a man from the outside can make him unclean?* [19] *For it doesn't go into his heart but into his stomach, and then out of his body.* (In saying this, Jesus declared all foods "clean.")" Mark 7:14-19 NIV. Notice the information in parenthesis at the end of

this passage of Scripture. The parenthesis means that this statement is not in the original manuscript but rather it was a translator's notation, a very ignorant one at that! Yahushua was not declaring all foods clean in this Scripture and He never made that statement. It is simply astounding that a translator would put such an erroneous notation at the end of a passage where the Messiah specifically asks "Are you so dull?" It is as if the Messiah is asking that question of the translator. The point of His teaching was that it is the heart that gets defiled, not the body. Eating something unclean does not turn someone into an unclean being. Eating pig does not turn a person into pig, they are still human. They do not turn into the unclean animal - instead their body eventually eliminates the unclean thing. Regardless, eating a pig is still considered an abominable act because swine is not defined as "food" in the Torah.

85 The problems which are found in many English translations is a subject addressed in the Walk in the Light series book entitled "Scriptures." It is important to make the distinction between the inerrancy of the Word and the inerrancy of a particular translation. In the present context I am only referring to errors made by human translators.

86 In a very strange way, the logic behind Dispensationalism is similar to that used by Evolutionists. Those that believe in evolution begin with the premise that there is no God and that they cannot rely on the Scriptural explanation for existence. Accordingly, they develop theories to show how mankind evolved from a one cell organism into human beings. Likewise, Dispensationalism promotes a form of spiritual evolution wherein mankind transcends from fallen man through a series of lesser species to the ultimate being - the Church. This type of thinking is under girded by anti-Semitism which views "Jews" as an inferior type of "spiritual subspecies." The writings of Martin Luther, Calvin and many other Christian Church fathers are replete with this notion. The fact of the matter is that there is no such thing as the "Church" as a new spiritual entity and it is absolutely contrary to Scriptures to try to explain away the "Jews"

and Yisrael through such baseless thinking. Just as school children are indoctrinated and inundated by evolutionary concepts from early age to the point where it becomes their accepted paradigm, and therefore an accepted truth through which they view life - the same can be said about Christians who were raised on Dispensational teaching. They read the Scriptures and view their existence and the existence of the "Church" through their inherited paradigm.

87 Genetic research has made it possible to discern the Y-Chromosome attributable to Cohanim and along with preparations to rebuild the Temple, there has naturally been a movement to identify and train the Priesthood. While writing this book I was in Jerusalem celebrating Sukkot and noticed a poster for a conference of Cohens and Levites. For further information on this issue see *DNA & Tradition* by Rabbi Yaakov Kleiman, Devora Publishing 2004.

88 There is so much that we can glean from this passage. The fact that YHWH put Avram to sleep immediately makes us think of Adam. If YHWH did not want Avram to see Him He could have easily told him not to look or even covered him like He did with Mosheh on Sinai. The fact that YHWH put him to sleep seems to raise a red flag and call special attention to this incident. I believe that it reflects the fact that YHWH was in the process of making for Himself a Bride through the Seed of Avraham and as He put Adam to sleep to take something out of him to create his bride - so He did the same with Avram, but instead of taking something out – YHWH added something to Avram which is symbolized in the hay (ה) which was later added to his name. Rabbi Yosef Kalatsky in a Beyond Pshat article provides the following commentary: "Based on a verse in Tehillim which alludes to the fact that Hashem [YHWH] formed the worlds with the letters "yud" and "hay," the Gemara in Tractate Menachos states, 'The physical world was created with the spirituality of the letter "hay" and the world to come was created with the spirituality of the letter "yud." Meaning, the spiritual energy contained within the letter "hay" brought about all physical existence. G-d said to Avraham, Just as the spiritual energy in the letter

"hay" was needed to bring about all physical existence, that same energy is needed to bring a change within you to be able to be the father, the Patriarch, of the Jewish people.' The additional "hay" is not merely another letter added to Avraham's name; but rather, it brought about a profound change within him; his dimension of person became the equivalent of all existence. Until the insertion of the letter "hay," Avraham had no relevance (as he was) to being the Patriarch of the Jewish people."
www.torah.org/learning/beyond-pshat/5764/vayera.html.
If YHWH (יהוה) did form the physical world with the (יה) which are the first two characters in His Name then one might reasonably ask - what about the last two letters of His Name. We can see the answer in the name of the first woman who is commonly called Eve, but her Hebrew name is Hawah (חוה). Her name means "life giver" and notice that it includes the last two letters of the Name of YHWH (וה). This life is not the same as the rest of creation which was already formed - this Life was the Life of YHWH which was breathed into Adam - it was what "made him in the image of YHWH." Now back to Avraham and Sarah - it is important to emphasize that there was not just one hay (ה) added - there were two. YHWH added one to the male Avraham and one to the female Sarah and when the two were joined together it was that Seed and that Womb which would provide the promised line from which Messiah would come forth. In my opinion, those two hays are the two hays found in the Name of YHWH (יהוה).

89 The Akida is the traditional name for the Torah portion involving the process of Avraham presenting his promised son as a sacrifice to YHWH. This portion establishes the pattern wherein YHWH would present His Son as a sacrifice.

90 Yitshaq (יצחק) is the correct transliteration for the Hebrew name commonly called Isaac.

91 We were previously shown the concept of covering after Eden when Adam and Hawah were covered by the dead animal skins but that was only a temporary covering - animals would

not suffice to restore Creation to its original state. What was needed was a perfect substitution to atone for their sin. That was the work of Messiah as the "Son of Adam" to obey as Adam failed and take the punishment for the transgression of Adam and his offspring. A common retort from Judaism is that Elohim does not condone human sacrifice and therefore the death of Yahushua is not sanctioned in the Scriptures. What must be made clear is that the death of Yahushua was not a human sacrifice at the Temple. If anything, it was a Roman sacrifice to their sun god as they sacrificed people on the cross of Tammuz. The point is that innocent blood was shed and some believe that blood actually fell on the Ark of the covenant which was hidden in a cave beneath the site of the crucifixion. (See www.wyattmuseum.com)

92 This is an incredibly significant occurrence which we need to learn from. The golden calf represented the worship of Hathor. Hathor was a popular Egyptian goddess associated with love, fertility, sexuality, music, dance and alcohol. Who better to invite to a party, at least that is what the Yisraelites thought as they proceeded to *"eat and drink and rise up to play."* (Shemot 32:6). They took some of what they knew and they said it was for YHWH. This is what Christianity commonly does with their holidays. Christmas and Easter are holidays with pagan roots but they have been "transformed" and made into festivals to YHWH. This is not acceptable worship of the Almighty.

93 It is well accepted that the successor of Mosheh, commonly called Joshua, was named Yahushau - the same name as the Messiah. This was by no means a coincidence but was a pattern established by the Almighy. If we look at the life of Joshua (Yahushua) we see a pattern for some of the things that Messiah would accomplish. Beyond His assistance to Mosheh and his participation in receiving the Torah, He circumcised the Yisraelites before they entered into the Promised Land. He lead Yisrael out of the Wilderness miraculously across the Jordan which was a symbolic baptism or rather tevila. He administered the first Passover in the Land and He fought giants in the land so that Yisrael

could settle the Land.

94 Contrary to popular Christian teaching, divorce is permitted in the eyes of YHWH, in particular when sexual misconduct has occurred and the parties are unable to reconcile. (Devarim 24:1). Many misapply the teaching of Yahushua in Mattityahu 19:3-9 as if He abolished divorce altogether. He specifically stated that He did not come to destroy the Torah so we know that His teachings did not change the Torah. What He was really doing was attacking the rules that men had developed which allowed them to divorce their wives for most any reason or send them away without divorcing them which created great difficulties for the woman who remained married and could not remarry without the divorce. (see Mattityahu 5:31).

95 The Sefer Hoshea gives an excellent example of how names are used by Elohim to demonstrate His purpose and plan. Hoshea was commanded to marry Gomer, a harlot. They had three children together named Jezreel, Lo-Ruhamah and Lo-Ammi. Jezreel is Yisre'el (יזרעאל) in Hebrew and means "El scatters" or "El sows." Lo-Ruhamah (לארחמה) means "no mercy" and Lo-Ammi (לעאימ) means "not my people." Therefore, YHWH was teaching that He would scatter the House of Yisrael, that He would not have mercy upon them, that they would then not be considered His people any longer and He would not be considered their Elohim. The prophesy does not stop there because He states that their numbers would be as the sand of the sea, a promise given to Avraham and Ya'akov. He then states that they would be gathered together with the House of Yahudah (Hoshea 1:11). This regathering is a prophesied event which has yet to occur. The marriage and subsequent redemption of Gomer is critical to understanding this prophesy. Hoshea, which means "salvation" is a clear reference to the Messiah and was the original name of Yahushua (Joshua) Son of Nun. He married a prostitute, which represents the House of Yisrael. Instead of remaining true to her Husband she continues to prostitute herself. Hoshea later redeems (purchases) her for a price (15 shekels of silver and one and one half omer of

barley). This is symbolic of the redemption that the Messiah pays for His Bride.

96 Yehezeqel (יהזקאל) is the proper Hebrew transliteration for the Prophet commonly called Ezekiel.

97 This is probably a good point to clarify that I am not suggesting that you have to join the religion of Judaism or become a citizen of the modern State of Israel to join Yisrael. Yisrael is not a religion, denomination, institution, organization, state or club – it is the Kingdom of YHWH.

98 The Creator's reckoning of time is discussed at length in the Walk in the Light series book entitled "Appointed Times." It is critical that anyone who claims to follow the Almighty understand His times and seasons in order to synchronize their lives with His plan.

99 In my opinion this added hey (ה) is the same hey added to Avram and Sarai. See Endnote 88.

100 A common teaching in Judaism is that the Gentiles are not required to obey the Torah – only the Seven Noahide Laws – which is a fabrication of the Rabbis. (Sanhedrin 56a; Rambam, Hil. Melachim 9:1). This is a tragedy. Gentiles are being told that they do not have to obey the Torah and in many cases told that they cannot obey the Torah unless they convert to Judaism. This, of course, is nonsense. You do not have to convert to any religion to obey the Torah – you simply need to join with Yisrael and "hold fast" to the covenant no matter what anyone tells you.

101 Nelson's Illustrated Bible Dictionary, Copyright (c)1986, Thomas Nelson Publishers - NOTE corrected names and spellings added for consistency and accuracy.

102 International Standard Bible Encyclopaedia, Electronic Database Copyright (c)1996 by Biblesoft.

103 I use the word altar loosely in this context because it is highly inappropriate to call the front of a Church Building an altar if you are referring to the Altar of YHWH. There is only one Altar in Heaven and the Torah specifically provides for an Altar at the Tabernacle. The practice of calling the front of a church an altar derives from pagan temples which, in large part, most Christian Church buildings mimic

architecturally.

104 The Christian religion has developed into a system which is not so concerned about the growth and development of its adherents as it is their numbers. It reminds me of an industrial veal farm which is focused on profit over the treatment of its members. And like a veal farm, it is a system which inhibits growth because it rarely allows Believers to exercise their spiritual muscles unless they are in a "leadership" position. So what we have is a bunch of weak, tender, milk fed calves that eat what is given to them every Sunday while they suffer from spiritual atrophy and wait to get slaughtered. Like veal, they live in a box which allows little to no movement or interaction with the outside - so there is no muscle growth. I am very concerned about this because I fear, from my own personal life experience, that many are ill prepared to face the difficult and challenging times that lay ahead for Believers. As long as you can maintain a structured life where you go to church and limit your interaction with adversarial beliefs - life may seem to be great. But when "all hell breaks loose" and your faith is shaken because someone who knows the Scriptures 100 times better than you shreds most of your core beliefs right before your eyes – that can be a pretty lonely place. That is why we are told to build on the Rock and that is why we need to break free from any system that hinders our growth and relationship with the Almighty by either hiding the truth or teaching and propagating lies.

105 If you examine the fabrication of the wilderness Tabernacle you will find many similarities to our bodies. It was a pattern and a demonstration of how we were to be living tabernacles (Shemot 36 - 38).

106 On this point I would encourage the reader to examine the Walk in the Light series book entitled "Kosher." It provides a concise, yet thorough apology for why every Believer should be observing the dietary instructions found within the Torah.

107 Rather than preparing to "endure to the end" many Christians have bought into the "escapist" mentality perpetrated by the Doctrine of the Rapture. Instead of learning how to live for

eternity they are biding their time until they get "raptured" which may happen at the very end, but it is not going to happen before the tribulation. The word "rapture" is not found within the Scriptures and the Pre-Tribulation Rapture is a fabricated doctrine like Dispensationalism. It can only be supported by twisting the text and pulling verses out of context. In my opinion it is so popular because it tickles the ears of those who are afraid of the future or because they don't have enough faith to believe that YHWH can see us through to the end. We are here on earth now – for a reason. If we get deluded into thinking that we just wait around until we are whisked away to glory then there will be many who will be unprepared to face the future.

108 For a more detailed discussion on the Sabbath I would recommend the Walk in the Light Series book entitled "The Sabbath."

109 To fully understand the plan of the Creator we must know His Appointed Times which are clearly described in the Torah. When we keep these appointments He meets with us and we are blessed. Just as Yahushua fulfilled the Torah by bringing fullness and meaning to the Feast of Pesach (Passover) and the Feast of Shavuot (Pentecost) – we await His fulfillment of the remaining Feasts. A more detailed discussion of the feasts may be found in the Walk in the Light series book entitled "Appointed Times."

Appendix A

Tanak Hebrew Names

Torah - Teaching

English Name	Hebrew	English Transliteration
Genesis	בראשית	Beresheet
Exodus	שמות	Shemot
Leviticus	ויקרא	Vayiqra
Numbers	במדבר	Bemidbar
Deuteronomy	דברים	Devarim

Nebi'im – Prophets

Joshua	יהושע	Yahushua
Judges	שופטים	Shoftim
Samuel	שמואל	Shemu'el
Kings	מלכים	Melakhim
Isaiah	ישעיהו	Yeshayahu
Jeremiah	ירמיהו	Yirmeyahu
Ezekiel	יחזקאל	Yehezqel
Daniel	דניאל	Daniel
Hosea	השוע	Hoshea
Joel	יואל	Yoel
Amos	עמוס	Amos
Obadiah	עבדיה	Ovadyah

Jonah	יונה	Yonah
Micah	מיכה	Mikhah
Nahum	נחום	Nachum
Habakkuk	חבקוק	Habaquq
Zephaniah	צפניה	Zepheniyah
Haggai	חגי	Chaggai
Zechariah	זכריה	Zekaryah
Malachi	מלאכי	Malachi

Kethubim – Writings

Psalms	תהלים	Tehillim
Proverbs	משלי	Mishle
Job	איוב	Iyov
Song of Songs	שיר השירים	Shir ha-Shirim
Ruth	רות	Ruth
Lamentations	איכה	Eikhah
Ecclesiastes	קהלת	Qohelet
Esther	אסתר	Ester
Ezra	עזרא	Ezra
Nehemiah	נחמיה	Nehemyah
Chronicles	דברי הימים	Divri ha-Yamim

Appendix B

The Walk in the Light Series

Book 1	Restoration - A discussion of the pagan influences that have mixed with the true faith through the ages which has resulted in the need for restoration. This book also examines true Scriptural restoration.
Book 2	Names - Discusses the True Name of the Creator and the Messiah as well as the significance of names in the Scriptures.
Book 3	Scriptures - Discusses the origin of the written Scriptures as well as many translation errors which have led to false doctrines in some mainline religions.
Book 4	Covenants - Discusses the progressive covenants between the Creator and His Creation as described in the Scriptures which reveals His plan for mankind.
Book 5	The Messiah - Discusses the prophetic promises and fulfillments of the Messiah and the True identity of the Redeemer of Yisra'el.
Book 6	The Redeemed - Discusses the relationship between Christianity and Judaism and reveals how the Scriptures identify True Believers. It reveals how the Christian doctrine of Replacement Theology has caused confusion as to how the Creator views the Children of Yisra'el.
Book 7	The Law and Grace - Discusses in depth the false

doctrine that Grace has done away with the Law and demonstrates the vital importance of obeying the commandments.

Book 8 The Sabbath - Discusses the importance of the Seventh Day Sabbath as well as the origins of the tradition concerning Sunday worship.

Book 9 Kosher - Discusses the importance of eating food prescribed by the Scriptures as a aspect of righteous living.

Book 10 Appointed Times - Discusses the appointed times established by the Creator, often erroneously considered to be "Jewish" holidays, and critical to the understanding of prophetic fulfillment of the Scriptural promises.

Book 11 Pagan Holidays - Discusses the pagan origins of some popular Christian holidays which have replaced the Appointed Times.

Book 12 The Final Shofar - Discusses the walk required by the Scriptures and prepares the Believer for the deceptions coming in the End of Days.

The series began as a simple Power point presentation which was intended to develop into a book with twelve different chapters but ended up being twelve different books. Each book is intended to stand alone although the series was originally intended to build from one section to another. Due to the urgency of certain topics, the books have not been published in sequential order.

For anticipated release dates, announcements and additional teachings go to:
www.shemayisrael.net

Appendix C

The Shema

Deuteronomy (Devarim) 6:4-5

Hear, O Israel: The LORD our God, the LORD is one! You shall love the LORD your God with all your heart, with all your soul, and with all your strength.

Traditional English Translation

שמצ ישראל יהוה אלהינו יהוה אחד
ואהבת את יהוה אלהיך בכל־ לבבך ובכל־ נפשך ובכל־ מאדך

Hebrew Text

Shema, Yisra'el: YHWH Elohenu, YHWH echad!
V-ahavta et YHWH Elohecha b-chol l'vavcha u-v-chol naf'sh'cha u-v-chol m'odecha.

Hebrew Text Transliterated

The Shema is arguably the most important prayer in Judaism and the Messiah stated that it was the First of all commandments. (Mark 12:29-30).

Appendix D

Shema Yisrael Foundation

The Shema Yisrael Foundation was established to promote Scriptural truth to the Nations of the World. This is accomplished by publishing articles and studies on the internet and in audio and written form including the Walk in the Light series. Also, Scriptures are provided to Believers around the world along with funds for food, shelter and clothing.

The foundation works in cooperation with other foundations and ministries to provide teaching and training to individuals around the world.

If you would like to help us achieve this goal you may do so through your prayers and financial contributions.

Please make checks payable to:

Shema Yisrael

Mail checks to:

Shema Yisrael
123 Court Street
Herkimer, New York 13350